PAIRING UP
2-BLOCK QUILTS

Nancy Mahoney

Martingale®
& COMPANY

Credits

President ■ Nancy J. Martin

CEO ■ Daniel J. Martin

Publisher ■ Jane Hamada

Editorial Director ■ Mary V. Green

Managing Editor ■ Tina Cook

Technical Editor ■ Cyndi Hershey

Copy Editor ■ Ellen Balstad

Design Director ■ Stan Green

Illustrator ■ Robin Strobel

Cover & Text Designer ■ Shelly Garrison

Photographer ■ Brent Kane

Mission Statement

Dedicated to providing quality products and service to inspire creativity.

That Patchwork Place® is an imprint of Martingale & Company®.

Pairing Up: 2-Block Quilts
© 2003 by Nancy Mahoney

Martingale & Company
20205 144th Avenue NE
Woodinville, WA 98072-8478 USA
www.martingale-pub.com

Printed in the USA
08 07 06 05 04 03   8 7 6 5 4 3 2 1

Library of Congress Cataloging-in-Publication Data

Mahoney, Nancy
    Pairing up: 2-block quilts/Nancy Mahoney.
        p. cm.
    ISBN 1-56477-489-9
    1. Patchwork—Patterns. 2. Quilting—Patterns I. Title.
    TT835.M342 2003
    746.46'041—dc21
                                                    2003008958

Dedication

To Tom, my knight in shining armor.

Acknowledgments

There are many people who supported and encouraged me in various ways while I wrote this book. A verbal "thank you" is hardly adequate for everyone, so I wish to extend special written thank-yous to the following people and companies:

- David Peha, owner of Clothworks/Fabric Sales Co., for his continuing support and friendship

- Julie Sheckman for the generous contribution of "Queen's Crossing"

- Machine quilters Barbara Dau, Jan Ogg, Susan Powell, and Jan Ulm. I can't thank them enough.

- The staff at Martingale & Company for their hard work, encouragement, and support

- Clothworks for fabric

- Free Spirit for fabric

- Hoffman Fabrics and Sandy Muckenthaler for fabric

- P & B Textiles and Julie Scribner for fabric

- Timeless Treasures and Emily Cohen for fabric

- American & Efird and Marci Brier for Mettler and Signature threads

- Hobbs Bonded Fibers and H. D. Wilbanks for batting

- Prym DritzOmnigrid for notions, rotary cutters, rulers, and mats

- The Electric Quilt Company for computer software

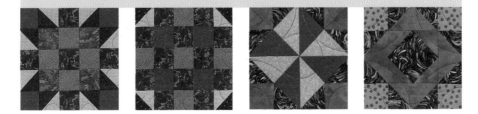

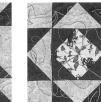

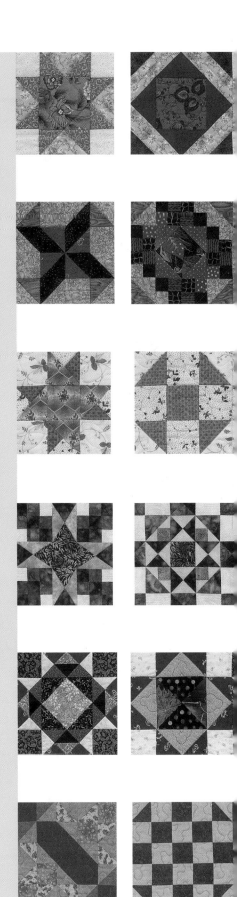

CONTENTS

Introduction ——————— 7

Supplies ————————— 8

Block Selection ————— 9

Blocks and Borders ——— 16

Fabric Selection ————— 17

Yardage Calculations ——— 18

Quiltmaking Basics ——— 19

The Quilts

    Peppermint Swirl ———— 34

    Cranberry Twist ———— 39

    Connect the Dots ———— 43

    Provence Garden ———— 48

    Fiesta ————————— 52

    Sirocco ———————— 57

    Sundance ——————— 64

    Queen's Crossing ———— 69

    Mulberry Road ———— 74

    Marble Mania ————— 79

    Golden Bough ————— 84

    Black Magic —————— 90

About the Author ———— 95

INTRODUCTION

I have always been fascinated by the secondary designs created when blocks are set side by side. The most common two-block quilts combine Nine Patch blocks with Snowball blocks. My first two-block quilts were also made with Snowball blocks, but I soon discovered that I wanted to take my designs to a new level. I began looking for traditional blocks that I could "pair up" to create quilts that would engage the viewer and create a visual puzzle.

Now you can unlock the mystery and start enjoying the fun of pairing up two different blocks to create your own unique quilts. You will make the viewer look at the whole quilt when you camouflage the point where one block ends and the other block begins. Spectacular quilts emerge from the interesting secondary designs created when you combine two different blocks in side-by-side settings.

This book includes step-by-step directions for 12 quilts, along with an alternate fabric plan for each of these 12 quilts. Several of the quilts require piecing templates, but most are composed entirely of squares, triangles, and rectangles. All of the quilts use one or more timesaving techniques for piecing the blocks. I encourage you to read the section on quiltmaking basics before beginning a project.

If you are a beginner, you may want to start with "Peppermint Swirl" on page 34, which combines an Ohio Star block with a Shoo Fly block. For quilters looking for more of a challenge, "Black Magic" on page 90 combines a World's Fair block with an Hour Glass Square block.

I hope that you will enjoy making the quilts in this book and that you will be challenged to stretch your imagination.

SUPPLIES

To make the quilts in this book, you will need the following supplies:

- 100%-cotton fabric as indicated for each quilt
- 100%-cotton thread
- Sewing machine in good working order
- Rotary-cutting equipment, including a rotary cutter, cutting mat, and a 6" x 24" acrylic ruler
- Fabric scissors
- Seam ripper
- Thin glass-head silk pins

Depending on the project, you might also need these supplies:

- Bias Square® ruler or other square ruler with a 45° line placed corner to corner
- Template plastic for making machine-piecing templates

BLOCK SELECTION

The first step to successful block selection and secondary patterns begins with looking at a block and dividing it visually into units. Most blocks are based on a grid, which can be defined as the number of squares into which a block is divided. To identify the correct grid for any grid-based block, count the number of divisions across the block. For example, a Four Patch block has two divisions; a Nine Patch block has three divisions. The most common grid-based blocks include Four Patch, Nine Patch, and Five Patch. They are generally easy to identify; easy to draw on graph paper; easy to modify to make new blocks; and best of all, easy to piece.

Once you are comfortable identifying a block's grid, pair up two different blocks that are based on the same grid. This way some of the intersections line up to create your secondary design. You'll want to select one block as the primary block and a second block as the connecting block. Usually the primary block is complex and has several pieces, while the connecting block is simpler and has fewer pieces. Once you select the blocks, use either graph paper or a quilt-related computer program to draw the primary and connecting blocks together in a side-by-side setting of five rows of five blocks. Disregard the block and seam lines when looking for new shapes and patterns to create the overall secondary design.

Balanced Designs

All four corners in symmetrical blocks are the same, creating a symmetrical or balanced design when used in odd-number combinations such as three rows of three blocks, five rows of five blocks, seven rows of five blocks, and so on. Asymmetrical blocks, which have opposite corners that are the same, create a symmetrical or balanced design when used in even-number combinations such as four rows of four blocks, six rows of six blocks, eight rows of six blocks, and so on.

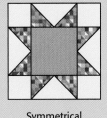

Symmetrical

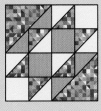

Asymmetrical

Two-Grid Block
(Four Patch)

Three-Grid Block
(Nine Patch)

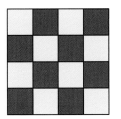

Four-Grid Block

Five-Grid Block

Two-Grid Blocks

The most common two-grid block is a Four Patch. Other examples are the Square within a Square block and the Broken Dishes block. Two-grid blocks can be used in combination to create four-grid and eight-grid blocks. When you combine the Broken Dishes block and Square within a Square block, a star emerges as the secondary pattern.

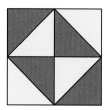

Broken Dishes

Square within a Square

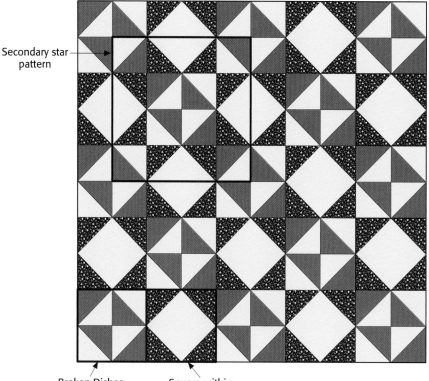

Secondary star pattern

Broken Dishes block

Square within a Square block

Three-Grid Blocks

Nine Patch, Shoo Fly, Ohio Star, and Garden Patch are all examples of three-grid blocks.

Although both quilts shown below have the same connecting block, the primary block is different, which gives each quilt a unique secondary pattern.

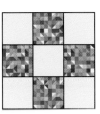

Nine Patch

Shoo Fly

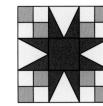

Ohio Star

Garden Patch

"Provence Garden" is made up of Garden Patch blocks and Shoo Fly blocks. See page 48 for a full-view photo of the quilt.

"Peppermint Swirl" is made up of Ohio Star blocks and Shoo Fly blocks. See page 34 for a full-view photo of the quilt.

11

Block Selection

Four-Grid Blocks

Most of the quilts in this book were designed using four-grid blocks. Blocks with several pieces increase the secondary-design possibilities. The blocks shown are examples of four-grid blocks. Notice that many of the blocks do not have a seam line in the center of the block.

As shown in the photo of "Golden Bough" below, the Crown of Thorns block is not easily recognized as a four-grid block until it is placed next to the Hour Glass Square block. In the photo of "Marble Mania," an asymmetrical Hovering Hawks block is combined with a symmetrical King's Crown block.

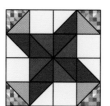

Whirling Pinwheel

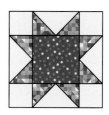

Sawtooth Star

Crown of Thorns

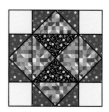

Hour Glass Square

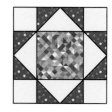

Hovering Hawks

King's Crown

Crown of Thorns blocks and Hour Glass Square blocks make up "Golden Bough." See page 84 for a full-view photo of the quilt.

"Marble Mania" is made with Hovering Hawks blocks and King's Crown blocks. See page 79 for a full-view photo of the quilt.

Five-Grid Blocks

The New England, Queen's Crown, and 'Round the Corner blocks are examples of five-grid blocks. Notice that Queen's Crown is an asymmetrical block.

As you can see in the photos that follow, 'Round the Corner is used as the connecting block in both quilts but with very different results.

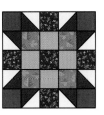

New England

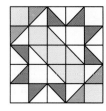

Queen's Crown

'Round the Corner

Queen's Crown blocks and 'Round the Corner blocks are featured in "Queen's Crossing." See page 69 for a full-view photo of the quilt.

Find New England blocks and 'Round the Corner blocks in "Mulberry Road." See page 74 for a full-view photo of the quilt.

Block Selection

Eight-Grid Blocks

Favorite Star and Stepping Stones are examples of eight-grid blocks. When the blocks are combined, the block lines are camouflaged successfully.

An eight-grid block is a division of a four-grid block, which means that four-grid and eight-grid blocks can be combined. However, depending on how the blocks meet at the intersecting points, the combination may or may not be successful.

On page 15, notice that a new block was produced from the Favorite Star block by dividing the rectangles and creating squares around the outer edges of the block. Making variations of a block by adding or subtracting lines can be an easy design solution to the problem of no intersecting points.

Favorite Star

Stepping Stones

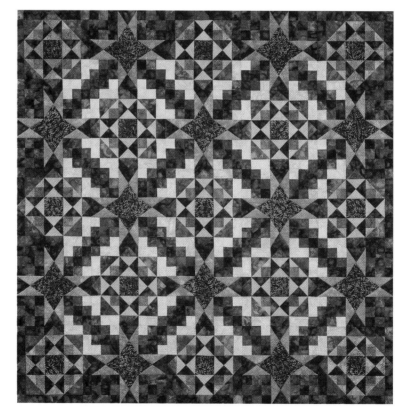

The quilt "Sirocco" is made with Favorite Star blocks and Stepping Stones blocks. See page 57 for a full-view photo of the quilt.

Favorite Star
Eight-Grid

Sawtooth Star
Four-Grid

Divide the rectangles
and create a new block.
Eight-Grid

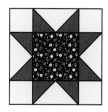

Sawtooth Star
Four-Grid

These two blocks are not a good pair
since they have no intersecting points.

Intersecting points give
the design more potential.

Favorite Star
Eight-Grid

Irish Chain
Four-Grid
(Eight-Grid Variation)

Divide the rectangles
and create a new block.
Eight-Grid

Irish Chain
Four-Grid
(Eight-Grid Variation)

3 intersecting points

Intersecting points create design possibilities.

5 intersecting points

With more intersecting points
the blocks blend together.

BLOCKS AND BORDERS

Another way to disguise blocks and add to the secondary design is to extend the blocks into the quilt border. "Sundance" on page 64 and "Golden Bough" on page 84 are examples of how the secondary designs were enhanced by extending the blocks into the inner border of the quilts. To help you visualize a design, make a line drawing of the blocks or project you want to create and draw in the borders. Look for lines that can be extended into the border. A word of caution: Some designs are easier to draw than to piece, so try to keep your design simple.

A simple way to create the look of a pieced border without any extra piecing is to change some of the fabrics in the blocks that are closest to the border. In "Sirocco" on page 57, the navy fabric used in the border replaces the pale yellow background in a section of the block. As a result, the line between the blocks and borders is disguised.

"Sirocco" Border

"Sundance" Border

"Golden Bough" Border

FABRIC SELECTION

The secondary design you create can vary dramatically depending on the type of fabrics you select and their placement. As with any quilt, value, or the relative lightness or darkness of a color, plays an important role. Repositioning light-value and dark-value fabrics can give a quilt design a completely different look.

Once you select the blocks or project that you want to sew and make a line drawing of your design on graph paper, use a pencil to add light, medium, and dark values to the design. Or if you have a quilt-related computer program, experiment with different color combinations. Either way, look for any secondary designs that you want to emphasize. The different color plans on page 18 illustrate how the look of a design changes depending on the position of light and dark values.

When you're ready to select fabrics for your quilt, start by choosing a multicolored print to use as the main fabric. Next, select a background fabric. Then decide which pieces in the design will be background fabrics and which will be the main fabric. Finally, for the remaining pieces in your quilt, use the main fabric to help you select other fabrics that will complete the fabric palette and complement the design.

Remember that the quilt's background fabric is as important as the rest of the fabrics in the quilt and can determine the mood of the quilt. The background fabric does not have to be a light value. I often use yellow or gold as my primary background fabric. Black is also a favorite choice and makes an excellent background for the rest of the fabrics in the quilt. I consider both yellow and black to be neutral colors, just like I view beige and cream.

To give you an idea about how different fabrics will change the look of a quilt, each project has an alternate fabric plan. Bear in mind that the number of fabrics required for the alternate fabric plan would be different from the materials required for the main project, and the yardage amounts and cutting instructions would also have to change. However, the construction and setting of the blocks are exactly the same.

A good example of how the amount of background area can change the look of a quilt is found by comparing "Mulberry Road" on page 74 and "Purple Passion" on page 78. "Mulberry Road" has very little background area and the stars disappear. "Purple Passion," however, has more background area and the stars break up the diagonal lines.

Other examples of different looks include "Queen's Crossing" on page 69, which uses two background fabrics of different values, and "Greenbriar" on page 73, which has only one background fabric. In "Greenbriar," the placement of the darkest value changes as well, making the diagonal lines less prominent. Another example is the background in "Cranberry Twist" on page 39, which changes from a tan fabric to a black fabric in "Orange Twist" on page 42 to make a dramatic difference.

"Fiesta" on page 52 doesn't have an actual background fabric, but the black print acts as a background to make the pinwheel float. In "Melrose Stars" on page 56, the black fabric plays a minor role, and along with the use of light-value fabrics, the pinwheels become less obvious and a different secondary design emerges.

Finally, compare "Black Magic" on page 90 and "Hazelnut Latte" on page 94. The positioning of light- and dark-value fabrics is reversed, creating a new puzzle for the viewer.

While the possibilities may not be limitless, be adventurous and try different fabrics and color combinations. Start with color combinations that you like, and then try to stretch your comfort zone. Don't feel obligated to stick with your initial selections. Make two of each block. If you like the results, make two more. If you don't like the results, decide which fabric needs to change. Before you make new blocks, place a piece of the new fabric on top of the fabric you want to change to see how the block will look. Then make the new blocks and save the old blocks for the back of the quilt. It's important to give yourself permission to experiment, try different options, and most of all, have fun.

Yardage Calculations

All of the projects in this book include yardage requirements. However, if you want to make an alternate-fabric-plan quilt, you will need to do a few calculations. The word calculations sounds a bit intimidating, but the process is not difficult.

For an example, refer to the first design option for the New England and 'Round the Corner blocks at right. First determine the number of pieces you need from each fabric. Let's start with the light fabric. There are 8 light 2" squares in the New England block and 13 New England blocks in the first design—8 times 13 equals 104 squares. Plus, there are 4 light 2" squares in the 'Round the Corner block and 12 blocks in this design—4 times 12 equals 48 squares. Add the two square totals together—104 plus 48 equals 152 light squares—for the total number of light 2" squares needed to make this quilt.

Next, to determine how many pieces can be cut from a width of light fabric, divide the width of the fabric by the size of each cut piece. If your fabric is 40" wide and the cut piece is 2" square, 40" divided by 2" equals 20 squares per 40" strip of fabric.

Then divide the total number of squares by the number of squares per 40" strip. In this case it's 152 divided by 20, which equals 7.6 strips. Round this number up to 8. Then multiply the number of strips by the size of the cut piece—8 strips times 2" square equals 16". Round 16" up to the nearest standard yardage measurement. You will need a minimum of 18" or ½ yard, but to allow for shrinkage and any errors in cutting you want to get at least ⅝ yard.

As a comparison, look at the second design at right for the same two blocks. The New England block has 5 light 2" squares (5 times 13 blocks equals 65 squares). The 'Round the Corner block has 4 light 2" squares (4 times 12 blocks equals 48 squares). The total number of light 2" squares is 113 (65 plus 48). The fabric width is 40" and the cut piece is 2" square; therefore, you can get 20 squares per 40" strip of fabric. Now divide the total number of squares by the number of squares per 40" strip—113 divided by 20 equals 5.6 (round up to 6 strips). Then multiply the number of strips by the size of the cut piece—6 times 2" equals 12". Now round 12" to the nearest standard yardage measurement. It just happens to be exactly ⅓

yard, but to allow for shrinkage and any cutting errors you want to purchase at least ⅜ yard.

Repeat these calculations for each fabric in the quilt. If the same fabric is used for both squares and triangles, complete the calculations separately for the squares and triangles, and then add the two totals to determine the amount needed of the specific fabric.

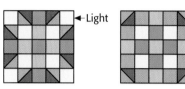

New England Block   'Round the Corner Block

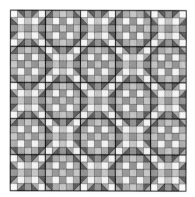

First Design

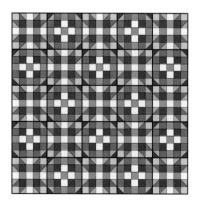

New England Block   'Round the Corner Block

Second Design

QUILTMAKING BASICS

On the pages that follow, you will find valuable information for the successful completion of your quilt. The timesaving techniques are a perfect reference tool for both beginners and experienced quiltmakers. Instructions for rotary cutting are provided whenever possible. If you are unfamiliar with rotary cutting, refer to Donna Lynn Thomas's *Shortcuts: A Concise Guide to Rotary Cutting* (That Patchwork Place, 1999) for rotary-cutting instructions. All measurements include ¼"-wide seam allowances.

Machine Piecing

The most important aspect in machine piecing is sewing an accurate ¼" seam allowance. This is necessary for the seams to match and the blocks to fit together properly. Some machines have a special presser foot that measures exactly ¼" from the center needle position to the edge of the foot. This allows you to align the edge of your fabric with the edge of the presser foot, resulting in a perfect ¼" seam allowance. On some machines, you can move the needle position to the right or left so that the resulting seam measures ¼" from the fabric edge to the stitching line.

If your machine doesn't have either of these features, you can create a seam guide by placing a piece of masking tape ¼" from the needle. Place an accurate ruler or piece of graph paper under the presser foot and lower the needle onto the seam line. Mark the seam allowance by placing a piece of masking tape at the edge of the ruler or paper. Use several layers of masking tape to build a raised edge to guide your fabric. Moleskin or a magnetic seam guide can also be used as a raised guide.

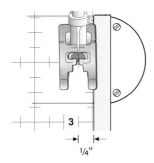

To test the accuracy of your ¼"-wide seam, follow these steps:

1. Cut two rectangles of fabric, each 1¼" x 3".

2. Sew the rectangles together, using the edge of the presser foot or the seam guide you have made. Press the seam flat and to one side. After sewing and pressing, the strip should measure exactly 2" wide. If it doesn't, adjust the needle or seam guide and sew another set of strips.

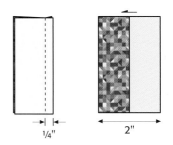

Chain Piecing

Chain piecing is an assembly-line method that lets you sew pieces together quickly. Rather than sewing each block from start to finish, you can sew units of each block together at one time, streamlining the process. It is recommended that you first sew one sample block together from start to finish to ensure the pieces have been cut accurately and that you have the proper positioning and coloration for each piece.

To start chain piecing, fold a thread-saver square in half and sew to its edge. Leave the presser foot down and feed the first pair of pieces under the presser foot. Sew from cut edge to cut edge. Stop sewing at the end of the piece but do not cut the thread. Feed the next pair of pieces under the presser

foot. Continue feeding pieces through the machine without cutting the thread. As you finish sewing the last piece, sew onto another thread saver. Leave the needle in place and the presser foot down on the thread saver. Cut the chain to remove the pieces from the machine. The thread saver will be in place to begin sewing the next unit or seam. Finally, take the connected units to the ironing board for pressing. Clip the threads between the sewn pieces as you press them.

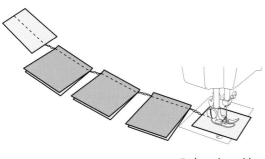

End sewing with a thread saver.

Sewing the Blocks

When sewing the fabric pieces that make up a unit or block, follow the piecing diagram provided for each block. Press each group of pieces before joining the group to the next unit.

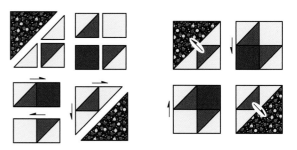

Stitch, and then press in the direction of the arrows.

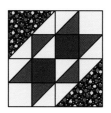

Stitch the units together.

Positioning Pins

A positioning pin will help you match two points. As shown in the triangle example below, insert a positioning pin through the back of the first triangle right at the tip of the triangle. Then pull the two triangle pairs far enough apart to see the tip of the second triangle and push the pin straight through the second triangle tip to establish the proper matching point. Note that you should not lock the positioning pin into the fabric; it should remain loose. Then place and lock a pin on either side of the positioning pin. Pin the remainder of the seam normally and remove the positioning pin before stitching.

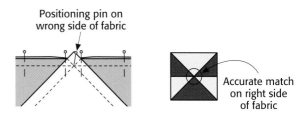

Positioning pin on wrong side of fabric

Accurate match on right side of fabric

The X Mark

When triangles are joined to other fabric pieces, the stitching lines cross each other on the back, creating an X at the seam line. Stitch through the center of the X to maintain a crisp point on your triangles.

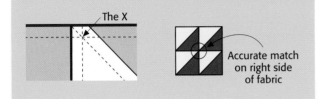

The X

Accurate match on right side of fabric

Opposing Seams

When stitching one unit to another unit, press seams that need to match in opposite directions. The two opposing seams will hold each other in place and evenly distribute the fabric bulk. Whenever possible, plan pressing to take advantage of opposing seams. You will find this especially important in strip piecing.

Accurate match on right side of fabric

Easing

When one piece is slightly longer than another and you must sew the two pieces together, you need to ease the pieces together when sewing. With the shorter piece on top, pin the points that need to match, the ends, and in between if necessary, to distribute the excess fabric. Stitch along the seam. The feed dogs, combined with a gentle tug, will ease the fullness of the longer piece to accommodate the top piece.

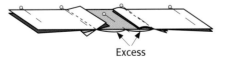

Excess

Removing Stitches and Resewing

Inspect each intersection from the right side to see if the seams match. If you decide to remove a line of stitching, use a seam ripper. To avoid stretching the fabric, cut the thread every three to four stitches on one side of the fabric. Then, on the reverse side, pull on the other thread to remove the stitches. Remove any small pieces of thread before restitching the seam.

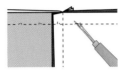

Pressing

Precise piecing is a combination of accurate cutting, sewing, and gentle pressing. After stitching a seam, it is important to carefully press your work. Pressing arrows are included in the project illustrations when it is necessary to press the seams in a specific direction. Following the arrows will help in constructing the blocks and assembling the quilt top. When no arrows are indicated, the direction in which you press the seam does not matter. In general, press seams toward the darker fabric or toward the section with fewer seams unless otherwise indicated.

Pressing Four-Patch Units

The following technique can be useful when joining four fabric pieces or units. You can create opposing seams and reduce the bulk where the seams come together. After the seam is sewn, use a seam ripper to remove one or two stitches from the seam allowance. Gently position both seam allowances to evenly distribute the fabric. Press the seams in opposite directions.

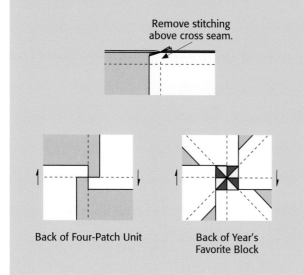

Back of Four-Patch Unit · Back of Year's Favorite Block

Making Half-Square- and Quarter-Square- Triangle Units

Many of the quilts in this book are made with half-square and quarter-square triangles. The difference between the two is the position of the straight grain (parallel to threads) and the bias (at an angle to the threads). On half-square triangles, the grain is on the short sides and the bias is on the long side. On quarter-square triangles, the grain is on the long side and the bias is on the short sides. It is important to recognize the difference in these pieces, because an edge that is cut on grain provides stability. An edge

that is cut on the bias is quite stretchy. Use the following quick methods for making multiple half-square and quarter-square triangle units.

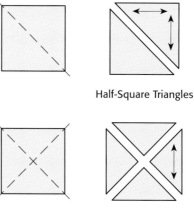

Half-Square Triangles

Quarter-Square Triangles

Half-Square-Triangle Units

Two half-square triangles sewn together to make a square is commonly called a half-square-triangle unit. The method described here is one of the easiest, fastest, and most accurate ways to make half-square-triangle units. Long bias strips are sewn together to make a strip set. Segments are cut from this strip set and the segments are cut into squares. The squares do not become distorted because the sewing and pressing are done *before* the squares are cut, avoiding any exposed bias edges.

1. Layer both fabrics with the right sides facing up.

2. Beginning at the corner of the fabrics, place a long ruler at a 45° angle to the bottom edge of the fabric. Cut along the edge of the ruler. Using the first cut as a guide, cut bias strips in the required

width for the quilt you are making. Continue to cut the strips across the entire fabric.

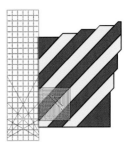

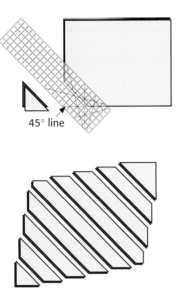

3. Separate and rearrange the strips, alternating the colors. You will have two sets of strips.

4. Sew the strips together along the bias edges, offsetting the point at the top edge ¼" as shown. Carefully press all seams toward the dark fabric.

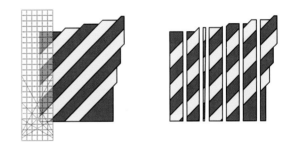

Sewn unit should have two even sides and two uneven sides.

5. Position a Bias Square ruler with the 45° angle on a seam line. Align the long cutting ruler with the edge of the Bias Square ruler so that the ends of

the strip are covered. Remove the Bias Square rule and trim the edge of the unit.

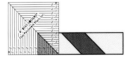

Place the 45° line of a ruler along a seam to accurately position the trimming ruler.

6. Cut a segment from the strip set the required width for the quilt you are making. Continue cutting segments, realigning the 45° diagonal line as needed. Maintaining a true 45° angle is critical to producing accurate units.

7. Using one cut segment, place the Bias Square ruler so that the edge of the ruler is even with the bottom edge of the fabric and the 45° diagonal line is along a seam line. Cut on the right side of the ruler. Continue cutting the segments, positioning the diagonal line of the ruler on each seam line.

8. Turn the cut segments (or mat) around to now place the right-hand cuts at the opposite end. Using one segment at a time, position the Bias Square ruler so that the edge of the ruler is even with the bottom edge of the fabric and the 45° line

Quiltmaking Basics

is along the seam line. Cut on the right side of the ruler to complete one half-square-triangle unit. Repeat with all segments.

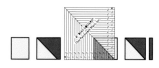

Quarter-Square-Triangle Units

This method is an easy, fast, and accurate way to make quarter-square-triangle units. Instead of sewing several individual triangles together, you sew long bias strips together to make half-square-triangle units. The sewing and pressing are done before the units are cut so that there is no distortion. The half-square-triangle unit is then cut in half diagonally to produce a quarter-square-triangle unit.

1. Follow steps 1–8 on pages 22–24 for making half-square-triangle units.

2. Cut one half-square-triangle unit on the diagonal to yield two quarter-square-triangle units.

Cut half-square-triangle units diagonally.

Recombine sections from two units.

Quarter-Square-Triangle Unit

Making Strip Sets

You can make multiple units more accurately and efficiently if you sew strips into strip sets and then cross-cut them into segments. By cutting with a rotary cutter, you can cut many pieces at the same time and eliminate the use of templates. For example, two strips are sewn together to make four-patch units for the Garden Patch blocks in "Provence Garden" on page 48, three strips are used to make nine-patch units for the Stepping Stones blocks in "Sirocco" on page 57, and four strips are joined to make the side units in the Irish Chain blocks in "Connect the Dots" on page 43. The following steps describe how to make strip sets for a four-patch unit, but you can use the same process for constructing other strip sets and units.

1. For a simple four-patch unit, cut the number of strips in the required width for the quilt you are making. Arrange the strips in the correct color combinations, with right sides together; sew the strips together along the long edges. Press the seams toward the dark fabric.

Make 2 strip sets.

2. Place one strip set on top of the other strip set, right sides together, with the light fabric on top of the dark fabric.

3. Trim the ends of the strip sets and cut the strip sets into segments. The width of each segment is specified in the directions for the quilt you are making.

4. Stitch the segment pairs together using a ¼"-wide seam allowance.

Four-Patch Unit

Making Flying-Geese Units

Several of the quilts in this book contain flying-geese units. The following steps describe a quick and easy way to make these units using squares and rectangles. It eliminates cutting triangles and at the same time is very accurate. Blocks that are made with flying-geese units include the Sawtooth Star and Around the Square.

1. On the wrong side of two squares, draw a diagonal line from corner to corner with the marking tool of your choice. If you are marking with a pen, use a permanent-ink pen; do not use a ballpoint pen.

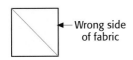

—Wrong side of fabric

2. Place a marked square on one end of a rectangle, right sides together and raw edges aligned. Stitch directly on the marked line. Trim away the excess fabric, leaving a ¼" seam allowance. Press the seam toward the square.

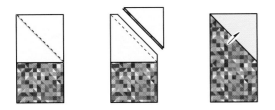

3. Place the second marked square on the other end of the rectangle, right sides together and raw edges aligned. Stitch directly on the marked line. Trim away the excess fabric, leaving a ¼" seam allowance. Press the seam toward the square.

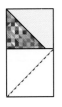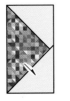

Flying-Geese Unit

Machine-Piecing Templates

The World's Fair, Stepping Stones, and Mosaic blocks have odd-shaped pieces that must be cut from fabric using piecing templates. To make templates, trace the provided patterns onto template plastic with a permanent-ink pen, making sure to trace the lines exactly. On the right side of the templates, mark the fabric grain line as shown on the patterns. All template patterns in this book include seam allowances. For future reference, you may also want to write the block name and piece letter on the template. Use utility scissors to cut out the templates, cutting exactly on the drawn lines. When placing templates on fabrics, pay careful attention to the grain line noted on each template. In many cases you will find it helpful to nest the template shapes across the fabric in order to make the best use of fabric.

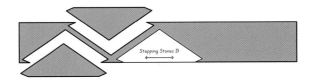

Stepping Stones B

Borders with Overlapped Corners

The simplest border to make is a border with overlapped corners. Most of the quilts in this book have this type of border. You will save fabric if you attach the border to the longer sides of the quilt top first, and then stitch the border to the remaining two sides. Yardage requirements for narrow borders (less than 2" wide) are based on cutting strips across the width of the fabric (unless noted otherwise) and joining them together for length. This is the most fabric-efficient way to cut narrow border strips.

Joining Crosswise Strips with a Diagonal Seam

To join cross-grained strips (cut across the width of the fabric) with a diagonal seam, sew the ends of the strips at right angles, with right sides together. Stitch across the diagonal and trim ¼" from the seam line. Join all the strips end to end to make one long continuous strip. Then measure the quilt top (see page 26), cut the borders from the long strip, and attach as directed.

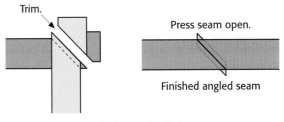

Trim.

Press seam open.

Finished angled seam

Piecing Border Strips

Measuring for Length of Border Strips

To find the correct measurement for the border strips, always measure through the center of the quilt, not at the outside edges. This ensures that the borders are of equal length on opposite sides of the quilt and brings the outer edges in line with the center dimension. Otherwise your quilt may not be square due to minor piecing variations. Refer to the following steps for detailed instructions.

1. Measure the length of the quilt top at the center. Cut two border strips to this measurement, piecing as necessary.

Measure center of
quilt, top to bottom.

2. Mark the center of the border strips and the quilt top. Pin the borders to the sides of the quilt top, matching centers and ends. Ease or slightly stretch the quilt to fit the border strip as necessary.

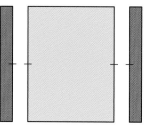

Mark centers.

3. Sew the side borders in place and press the seams toward the border strip.

4. Measure the center width of the quilt top, including the side borders, to determine the length of the top and bottom border strips. Cut two border strips to this measurement, piecing as necessary. Mark the center of the border strips and the quilt top. Pin the borders to the top and bottom of the quilt top, matching centers and ends. Ease or slightly stretch the quilt to fit the border strip as necessary.

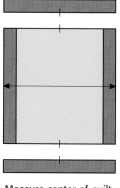

Measure center of quilt,
side to side, including
borders. Mark centers.

5. Sew the top and bottom borders in place and press the seams toward the border strips.

Borders with Mitered Corners

Mitered borders have a diagonal seam where the borders meet in the corners. There are certain fabrics that look better when used in borders with mitered corners. If your quilt has multiple borders and you plan to sew mitered corners, first sew the individual border strips together and treat the resulting unit as a single border strip. Refer to the following steps for detailed mitered-border instructions.

A Mitered Corner

1. First estimate the finished outside dimensions of your quilt, including the borders. Border strips should be cut to this length plus at least ½" for seam allowances. To be safe, give yourself some leeway by adding 3" to 4".

2. Mark the center of the quilt edges and the border strips.

3. Measure the length and width of the quilt top across the center.

4. Place a pin at each end of the side border strips equidistant from the center to mark the length of the quilt top. Repeat with the top and bottom borders.

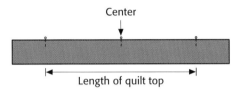

Center

Length of quilt top

5. Pin the borders to the quilt top, matching the centers. Line up the pins at either end of each border strip with the quilt edges, and pin the border to the quilt. Stitch, beginning and ending the stitching ¼" from the raw edges of the quilt top. Repeat with the remaining borders. Press seams toward the borders.

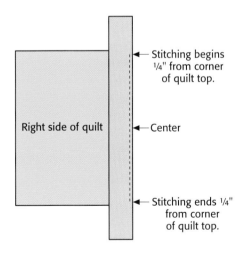

Stitching begins ¼" from corner of quilt top.

Right side of quilt

Center

Stitching ends ¼" from corner of quilt top.

6. Lay the first corner to be mitered on an ironing board. Fold under one border strip at a 45° angle to the other strip. Check that the outside corner is a 90° angle. Press the fold and pin in place as shown.

7. Fold the quilt top with the right sides together, lining up the edges of the border. If necessary, use a ruler and pencil to draw a line on the pressed crease to make the line more visible. Stitch directly on the crease, sewing away from the corner toward the outside edges.

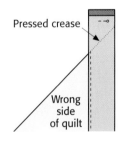

Pressed crease

Wrong side of quilt

8. Trim away excess border strips, leaving a ¼"-wide seam allowance. Press the seam open.

9. Repeat with the remaining corners.

Making the Backing

Every quilt consists of three layers—the quilt top, backing, and batting. To make your quilt backing, cut a piece of fabric 2" to 4" larger than the quilt top all the way around. For quilts larger than crib size, you will need to piece the backing from two or more widths of fabric if you use 42"-wide fabric. The seam can run horizontally or vertically unless the fabric is a print that is best viewed from a specific direction. When piecing the backing, be sure to trim off the selvages before sewing the pieces together. Press the seam open to reduce the bulk.

If your backing is just a little too narrow for the quilt top, you can solve this annoying problem with a little creative piecing. Some methods take more time than others, but pieced backs can be fun to make and constructed with leftover quilt-top fabrics or blocks.

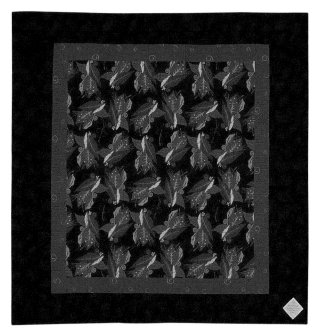

Back of "Connect the Dots"

Back of "Fiesta"

Preparing the Batting

There are many types of batting to choose from. The type of batting you choose will depend on whether you plan to hand or machine quilt your quilt top. Generally the thinner the batting—either cotton or polyester—the easier it is to hand quilt. For machine quilting you may want to use cotton batting that has a scrim, or thin mesh, that the fibers are woven through. A scrim helps stabilize the batting so that quilting lines can be farther apart, but it can be difficult to hand quilt. You can buy batting by the yard or purchase it packaged in standard bed sizes. If you are using prepackaged batting, open the package and smooth the batting out flat. Allow the batting to rest in this position for at least 24 hours. Also allow 2" of extra batting around all edges of the quilt top.

Layering the Quilt

To put all the quilt layers together—quilt top, backing, and batting—follow these steps:

1. Spread a well—pressed backing, wrong side up, on a flat, clean surface. Anchor it with pins or masking tape. Be careful not to stretch the backing out of shape.

2. Spread the batting over the backing, smoothing out any wrinkles.

3. Place the pressed quilt top, right side up, on top of the batting. Smooth out any wrinkles and make sure the edges of the quilt top are parallel to the edges of the backing. Smooth from the center out and along straight lines to ensure that the edges remain straight.

4. For hand quilting, baste with needle and thread, starting in the center and working diagonally to each corner. Continue basting in a grid of horizontal and vertical lines 6" to 8" apart. To finish, baste around the edges, about ⅛" from the edge of the quilt top.

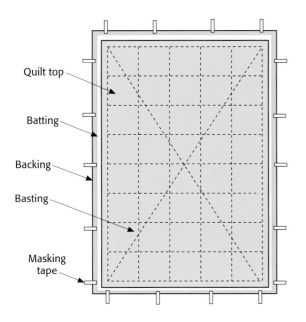

Quilt top
Batting
Backing
Basting
Masking tape

For machine quilting, baste the layers with #2 rustproof safety pins. Place pins 4" to 6" apart; try to avoid areas where you intend to quilt.

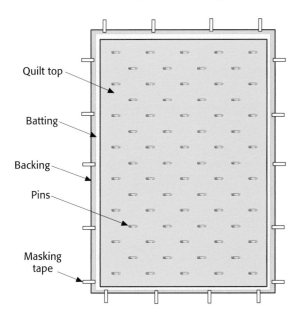

Quilt top
Batting
Backing
Pins
Masking tape

Quilting

When deciding on your quilting designs, consider the desired effect. The quilting design can add to the overall secondary design of your quilt. As a rule, the quilting should always enhance the quilt rather than distract the viewer.

The two most common forms of quilting are quilting in the ditch and outline quilting. Both can be done either by hand or by machine. To decide how much quilting is needed, use the general rule that any unquilted spaces should be no bigger than 4" x 4". The amount of quilting should be similar throughout the entire quilt so that the quilt will remain square and not become distorted. A common mistake is to heavily quilt the center of a quilt top and do very little quilting in the border.

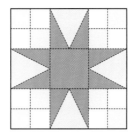

Quilting in the Ditch

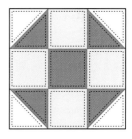

Outline Quilting

In this close-up view of "Sundance," you can see quilting in the ditch and stippling.

Quiltmaking Basics

Hand Quilting

To quilt by hand, you will need short, sturdy needles (called Betweens), quilting thread, and a thimble to fit the middle finger of your sewing hand. Most quilters use a frame or hoop to support their work. Use the smallest needle you can comfortably handle; the finer the needle, the smaller your stitches will be.

1. Thread your needle with a single strand of quilting thread about 18" long. Make a small knot and insert the needle in the top layer about 1" from the point where you want to start stitching. Pull the needle out at the point where quilting will begin and gently pull the thread until the knot pops through the fabric and into the batting.

2. Place one hand underneath the quilt so that you can feel the point of the needle with the tip of your first finger when a stitch is taken. Take small, evenly spaced stitches through all three layers. Rock the needle up and down until you have three or four stitches on the needle.

3. To end a line of quilting, make a small knot close to the last stitch; then backstitch, running the thread a needle's length through the batting. Gently pull the thread until the knot pops into the batting; clip the thread at the quilt's surface.

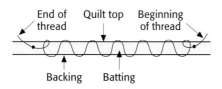

End of thread · Quilt top · Beginning of thread

Backing · Batting

Machine Quilting

Machine quilting is suitable for all types and sizes of quilts and allows you to complete a quilt quickly.

For straight-line quilting, it is extremely helpful to have a walking foot to help feed the layers through the machine without shifting or puckering. Some machines have a built-in walking foot; other machines require a separate attachment.

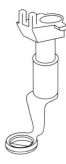

Walking Foot Attachment   Darning Foot

For free-motion quilting, you need a darning foot and the ability to drop the feed dogs on your machine. With free-motion quilting, you do not turn the fabric under the needle but instead guide the fabric in the direction of the design. Because the feed dogs are lowered, the stitch length is determined by the speed at which you run the machine and feed the fabric under the foot. Use free-motion quilting to outline a quilt pattern in the fabric or to create stippling and many other designs.

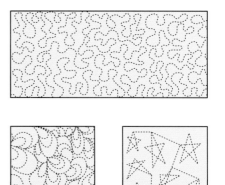

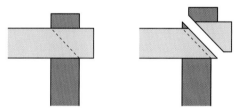

Quilting Practice

Before you begin machine quilting your quilt top, make a sample square consisting of two 6" squares of fabric and a 6" square of batting. Practice moving the fabric with your hands and controlling the machine's speed until you feel comfortable and can sew even stitches.

Squaring Up a Quilt

When you complete the quilting, you will need to square up your quilt before sewing on the binding. Align a ruler with the seam line of the outer border and measure the width of the outer border in several places. Using the narrowest measurement, position a ruler along the seam line of the outer border and trim the excess batting and backing from all four sides. At each corner, use a large square ruler to square up the corners.

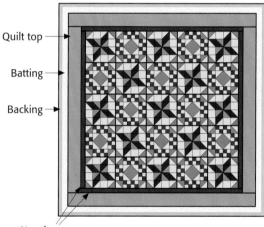

Quilt top

Batting

Backing

Use these seam lines as a guide.

Binding

The binding is your last chance to add to the overall look of the quilt. If you want the binding to disappear, then use the same fabric for the binding as the outer border. If you prefer for the binding to frame the outer border or become an additional border, then use a fabric that is different from the outer border. The binding can also be made from leftover strips, provided the strips are the correct width or can be cut down to the desired width. Whatever you choose, it should complement the quilt top.

I prefer a double-fold binding made from straight-grain strips. A straight-grain binding is easier to work with and takes less fabric than a bias-cut binding. I also cut 2"-wide strips for my binding. Depending on your batting choice, you may want to cut the strips wider. You will need enough strips to go around the perimeter of the quilt plus about 10" for seams and turning corners. The number of strips is specified for each quilt. If you are going to attach a sleeve to the back of your quilt for hanging, turn to "Adding a Sleeve" on page 33 and attach it now, before you bind the edges.

1. Cut 2"-wide strips across the width of the fabric as required for your quilt.

2. Join the strips at right angles and stitch across the corner as shown. Trim the excess fabric, leaving a ¼" seam allowance, and press the seams open.

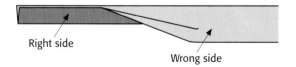

3. Fold the binding in half lengthwise, with the wrong sides together, and press.

Right side

Wrong side

Quiltmaking Basics

4. Unfold the binding at one end and turn under ¼" at a 45° angle as shown.

Fold line

5. Starting on the bottom edge of the quilt, stitch the binding to the quilt. Use a ¼" seam allowance. Begin stitching 3" from the start of the binding. Stop stitching ¼" from the first corner and back-stitch.

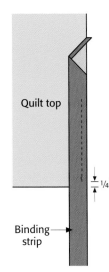

Quilt top

¼"

Binding strip

6. Remove the quilt from the sewing machine. Fold the binding away from the quilt, and then fold again as shown to create an angled pleat at the corner.

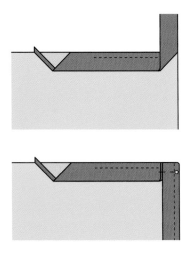

7. Start stitching at the fold of the binding. Backstitch at the beginning of the seam and then continue stitching along the edge of the quilt top. Stop ¼" from the next corner and backstitch. Repeat step 6 to form another mitered corner. Continue stitching around the quilt, repeating the mitering process at each corner.

8. When you reach the beginning of the binding, stop 3" before the starting end and backstitch. Remove the quilt from the machine. Trim the end 1" longer than needed and tuck the end inside the beginning strip. Pin in place, making sure the strip lies flat. Stitch the rest of the binding.

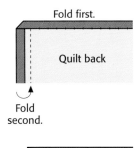

9. Turn the binding to the back of the quilt. Hand stitch the binding in place with the folded edge covering the row of machine stitching. Use thread that matches the binding. At each corner, fold the binding to form a miter on the back of the quilt.

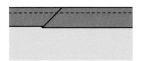

Fold first.

Quilt back

Fold second.

Adding a Sleeve

If you plan to hang your quilt, attach a sleeve or rod pocket to the back before attaching the binding. From the leftover backing fabric, cut an 8"-wide strip of fabric equal to the width of your quilt. You may need to piece two or three strips together for larger quilts.

1. On each end of the strip, fold over ½" and then fold ½" again. Press and stitch by machine.

½" ½"

2. Fold the strip in half lengthwise, wrong sides together; baste the raw edges to the top edge of the back of your quilt. These will be secured when you sew on the binding. Your quilt should be about 1" wider than the sleeve on both sides.

3. Make a little pleat in the sleeve to accommodate the thickness of the rod, and then slipstitch the ends and bottom edge of the sleeve to the backing fabric. This keeps the rod from being inserted next to the quilt backing.

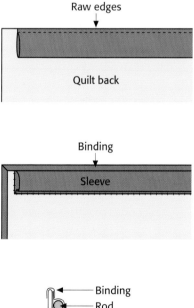

Raw edges

Quilt back

Binding

Sleeve

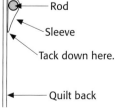

Binding

Rod

Sleeve

Tack down here.

Quilt back

Adding a Label

Future generations will want to know who made your quilt. A label provides important information including the name of the quilt, who made it, when, and where. You may also want to include the name of the recipient if it is a gift and any other interesting or important information about the quilt.

A label can be as elaborate or as simple as you desire. To make a label, use a permanent-ink pen to write all of the information on a piece of muslin or light-colored fabric. Press a piece of freezer paper to the back of the muslin to stabilize it while you write. To help you write straight, draw lines on the freezer paper with a fat-tipped marker as a guide. You should be able to see the lines through the fabric.

When the label is complete, remove the freezer paper and press the raw edges to the wrong side of the label. Stitch the label to the lower-right corner of the back of the quilt with a blind hem stitch.

Label from "Connect the Dots"

Quiltmaking Basics

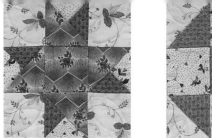

Ohio Star   Shoo Fly

PEPPERMINT SWIRL

Materials

Yardage is based on 42"-wide fabric.

- 1⅜ yards of pink print for Ohio Star and Shoo Fly blocks, outer border, and binding
- ⅞ yard of light floral print A for Ohio Star and Shoo Fly blocks
- ⅞ yard of light floral print B for Ohio Star blocks, Shoo Fly blocks, and inner border
- ½ yard of blue print for Ohio Star blocks and inner border
- 1 fat quarter *each* of 5 pink prints for Ohio Star and Shoo Fly blocks
- 1 fat quarter *each* of 3 blue prints for Ohio Star blocks
- 2½ yards of fabric for backing (If the backing fabric is wide enough, 1¼ yards of fabric may be enough.)
- 44" x 44" piece of batting

Cutting

All measurements include ¼" seam allowances.

From *each* of the 3 blue fat quarters, cut:

2 squares, 8" x 8" (6 total)

From the ½ yard of blue print, cut:

1 square, 8" x 8"

4 strips, 1½" x 42"; crosscut *each* of 2 strips into two 1½" x 8½" rectangles, one 1½" x 9½" rectangle, and one 1½" x 10½" rectangle. Crosscut 1 strip into 2 rectangles, 1½" x 9½", and 2 rectangles, 1½" x 10½". Crosscut 1 strip into 16 squares, 1½" x 1½".

From light floral print B, cut:

3 strips, 2½" x 42"; crosscut into 48 squares, 2½" x 2½"

2 strips, 8" x 42"; crosscut into 7 squares, 8" x 8"

1 strip, 1½" x 42"; crosscut into 8 rectangles, 1½" x 2½"

From *each* of the 5 pink fat quarters, cut:

4 squares, 2½" x 2½" (20 total)

4 squares, 2⅞" x 2⅞" (20 total); cut each square in half once diagonally to yield 40 half-square triangles

1 square, 8" x 8" (5 total)

From the 1⅜ yards of pink print, cut:

4 strips, 4" x 42"

5 strips, 2" x 42"

5 squares, 2½" x 2½"

6 squares, 2⅞" x 2⅞"; cut each square in half once diagonally to yield 12 half-square triangles

1 square, 8" x 8"

From light floral print A, cut:

2 strips, 8" x 42"; crosscut into 6 squares, 8" x 8"

4 strips, 2½" x 42"; crosscut into 52 squares, 2½" x 2½"

"Peppermint Swirl" by Nancy Mahoney. The Shoo Fly blocks extend into the inner border, creating the illusion that the blocks are set on point.

Finished Quilt Size: 39½" x 39½" ■ *Finished Block Size: 6"*

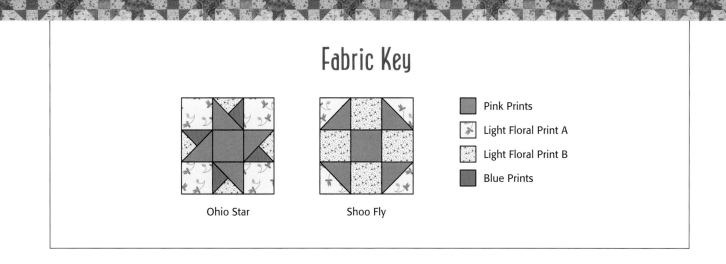

Fabric Key

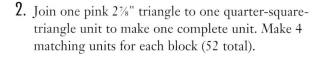

Pink Prints	
Light Floral Print A	
Light Floral Print B	
Blue Prints	

Ohio Star   Shoo Fly

Ohio Star Blocks

1. Pair each 8" square of blue print with each 8" square of light floral print B, right sides facing up. Cut and piece 3"-wide bias strips, following the directions on page 22 for making half-square-triangle units. Make 13 strip sets. Cut 52 half-square-triangle units, each 2⅞" x 2⅞". Crosscut each unit on the diagonal to yield quarter-square-triangle units (see page 24 for making quarter-square-triangle units). Only one quarter-square-triangle unit from each half-square-triangle unit is needed for this block.

NOTE: Since only half of the quarter-square-triangle units are being used in this quilt, you may prefer a different method of making these units. I prefer the Bias Square method for its accuracy.

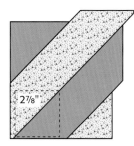

Make 13 strip sets.
Cut 52 units.

Use this half only.

Set this
half aside.

Make 4 matching
units for each block
(52 total).

2. Join one pink 2⅞" triangle to one quarter-square-triangle unit to make one complete unit. Make 4 matching units for each block (52 total).

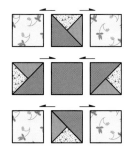

Make 4 matching
units for each block
(52 total).

3. Join four matching triangle units, a 2½" square from the same pink print, and four 2½" squares of light floral print A into rows. Press. Join the rows to make one Ohio Star block. Press. Make 13 blocks.

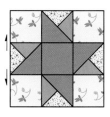

Make 13.

Shoo Fly Blocks

1. Pair each 8" square of pink print with each 8" square of light floral print A, right sides facing up. Cut and piece 2½"-wide bias strips, following the directions on page 22 for making half-square-triangle units. Make 12 strip sets. Cut 48 half-square-triangle units, each 2½" x 2½".

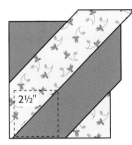

Make 12 strip sets.
Cut 48 units.

2. Join four matching half-square-triangle units, a 2½" square from the same pink print, and four 2½" squares of light floral print B into rows. Press. Join rows to make one Shoo Fly block. Press. Make 12 blocks.

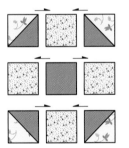
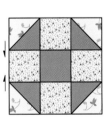

Make 12.

Quilt-Top Assembly

1. Arrange and sew the blocks together in five rows of five blocks each, alternating the Ohio Star and Shoo Fly blocks. Press.

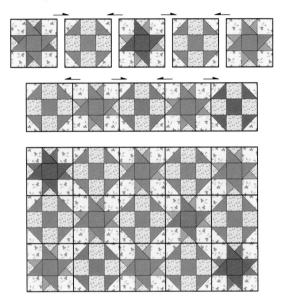

NOTE: The quilt top must measure 30½" x 30½" at this point in order for the pieced border to fit properly.

2. For the inner-border strips, refer to "Making Flying-Geese Units" on page 24. Join two 1½" squares of blue print to one rectangle, 1½" x 2½", of light floral print B to make one unit. Press.

Make 8 matching
flying-geese units.

3. Join two blue-print 1½" x 8½" rectangles, one blue-print 1½" x 10½" rectangle, and two flying-geese units to make one side inner border. Press. Repeat.

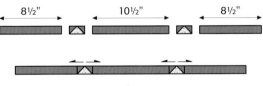

Make 2.

Peppermint Swirl

4. Join two blue-print 1½" x 9½" rectangles, one blue-print 1½" x 10½" rectangle, and two flying-geese units to make one top inner-border strip. Press. Repeat for the bottom inner-border strip.

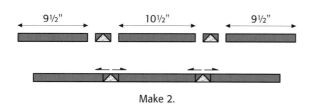

Make 2.

5. Referring to "Borders with Overlapped Corners" on pages 25–26, sew the inner-border strips to the side edges of the quilt top first, and then to the top and bottom edges. Press.

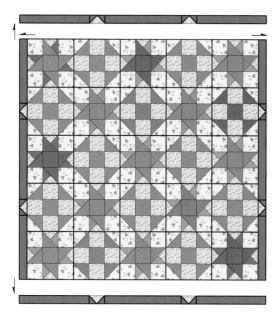

6. Referring to "Borders with Overlapped Corners" on pages 25–26, measure and cut the outer-border strips and sew them to the side edges of the quilt top first, and then to the top and bottom edges.

Finishing

1. Referring to "Layering the Quilt" on pages 28–29, layer the quilt top with batting and backing. Baste.

2. Referring to "Quilting" on page 29, quilt straight lines in the ditch and a motif in the background areas.

3. Referring to "Squaring Up a Quilt" on page 31, square up the quilt sandwich.

4. Referring to "Binding" on pages 31–32, prepare and sew the binding to the quilt.

Alternate Fabric Plan

See the lattice you can create when you change one of the background fabrics to a darker value than the other background fabric.

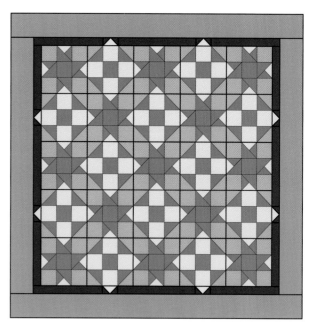

"Leaping Frogs"

Year's Favorite

Around the Square

CRANBERRY TWIST

Materials

Yardage is based on 42"-wide fabric.

- 2⅝ yards of red print A for Around the Square and Year's Favorite blocks, inner and outer borders, and binding
- 1⅝ yards of tan print for Around the Square and Year's Favorite blocks
- ¾ yard of red print B for Around the Square and Year's Favorite blocks
- ⅝ yard of floral print for Around the Square blocks and middle border
- 3½ yards of fabric for backing
- 60" x 60" piece of batting

Cutting

All measurements include ¼" seam allowances.

From the tan print, cut:

7 strips, 2½" x 42"; crosscut into 100 squares, 2½" x 2½"

6 strips, 2½" x 42"; crosscut into 48 rectangles, 2½" x 4½"

4 pieces, 18" x 21"; crosscut 1 piece into 48 squares, 2½" x 2½"

From red print B, cut:

1 strip, 2⅞" x 42"; crosscut into 12 squares, 2⅞" x 2⅞". Cut once diagonally to yield 24 half-square triangles.

2 pieces, 18" x 21"; crosscut 1 piece into 48 squares, 2½" x 2½"

From red print A, cut in order:

2 pieces, 18" x 21", from the crosswise grain

6 strips, 2" x 42", from the crosswise grain

4 strips, 2" x the remaining lengthwise grain

4 strips, 4½" x the remaining lengthwise grain

48 squares, 2½" x 2½", from the remaining width of fabric

12 squares, 2⅞" x 2⅞", from the remaining width of fabric; cut once diagonally to yield 24 half-square triangles

From the floral print, cut:

1 strip, 3⅜" x 42"; crosscut into 12 squares, 3⅜" x 3⅜"

5 strips, 2½" x 42"

39

"Cranberry Twist" by Nancy Mahoney. Machine quilted by Jan Ulm. By using one background print, the Year's Favorite and Around the Square blocks merge and appear to twist around the floral squares.

Finished Quilt Size: 55½" x 55½" ■ *Finished Block Size: 8"*

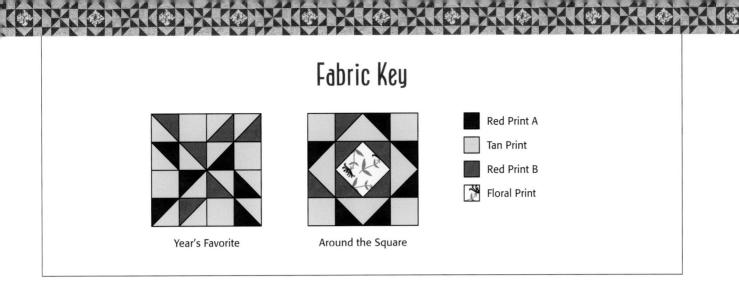

Fabric Key

■ Red Print A
□ Tan Print
■ Red Print B
❀ Floral Print

Year's Favorite

Around the Square

Year's Favorite Blocks

1. Pair each 18" x 21" piece of tan print with an 18" x 21" piece of red print A or B, right sides facing up. Cut and piece 2½"-wide bias strips, following the directions on page 22 for making half-square-triangle units. Make 5 strip sets. Cut 156 half-square-triangle units, each 2½" x 2½".

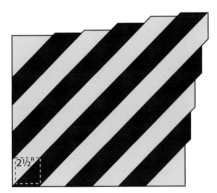

Make 5 strip sets.
Cut 156 units.

2. Join three half-square-triangle units and one tan 2½" square to make a quarter of the block. Refer to "Pressing Four-Patch Units" on page 22 for tips on pressing the center seams to reduce the bulk. Make 4 quarter units for each block (52 total).

Make 52.

3. Join four of the quarter units to make one Year's Favorite block. Refer to "Pressing Four-Patch Units" on page 22 for tips on pressing the center seams to reduce the bulk in the center of the block. Make 13 blocks.

Make 13.

Around the Square Blocks

1. Referring to the directions on page 24 for making flying-geese units, join two red 2½" squares to one tan rectangle to make one side unit. Press. Make 4 side units for each block (48 total).

Make 48.

2. Join four matching red 2⅞" triangles to one floral 3⅜" square to make one center unit. Press. Make 1 unit for each block (12 total).

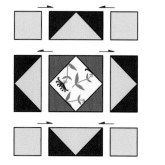

Make 12.

3. Join four tan 2½" squares, four side units, and one center unit into rows. Press. Join rows to make one Around the Square block. Press. Make 12 blocks.

Make 12.

Quilt-Top Assembly

1. Arrange and sew the blocks together in five rows of five blocks each, alternating the Year's Favorite and Around the Square blocks. Press. Join the rows. Press.

2. Referring to "Borders with Overlapped Corners" on pages 25–26, measure and cut the inner-border 2"-wide strips from red print A (cut from the lengthwise grain) and sew them to the side edges of the quilt top first, and then to the top and bottom edges. Press. Repeat for the middle-border strips from the floral print and the outer-border 4½"-wide strips from red print A.

Finishing

1. Referring to "Layering the Quilt" on pages 28–29, layer the quilt top with the batting and backing. Baste.

2. Referring to "Quilting" on page 29, quilt with an allover pattern.

3. Referring to "Squaring Up a Quilt" on page 31, square up the quilt sandwich.

4. Referring to "Binding" on pages 31–32, prepare and sew the binding to the quilt.

Alternate Fabric Plan

The orange stars and black background give this design a new twist.

"Orange Twist"

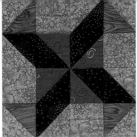

Whirling Pinwheel　　　**Irish Chain**

Connect the Dots

Materials

Yardage is based on 42"-wide fabric.

- 2¼ yards of gold for Irish Chain and Whirling Pinwheel blocks
- 2 yards of leaf print with black background for Irish Chain blocks and border
- 1⅝ yards of black with purple dots for Whirling Pinwheel blocks and binding
- 1⅛ yards of blue for Irish Chain and Whirling Pinwheel blocks
- ⅝ yard of purple A for Whirling Pinwheel blocks
- ½ yard of purple B for Irish Chain blocks
- ⅜ yard of black with red dots for Irish Chain blocks
- ⅜ yard of black plaid for Irish Chain blocks
- ⅜ yard of black-and-red stripe for Irish Chain blocks
- ¼ yard of red dot for Irish Chain blocks
- 4 yards of fabric for backing
- 65" x 65" piece of batting

Cutting

All measurements include ¼" seam allowances.

From purple A, cut:

2 pieces, 18" x 21"

From the black with purple dots, cut:

7 strips, 2" x 42"

4 pieces, 18" x 21"

From the gold, cut:

4 strips, 3" x 42"; crosscut into 52 squares, 3" x 3"

3 strips, 1¾" x 42"

5 pieces, 18" x 21"

From the blue, cut:

3 pieces, 18" x 21"

From the red dot, cut:

3 strips, 1¾" x 42"

From *each* of the black-and-red stripe, black plaid, and black with red dots, cut:

6 strips, 1¾" x 42" (18 total)

From purple B, cut:

3 strips, 3⅜" x 42"; crosscut into 24 squares, 3⅜" x 3⅜". Cut each square in half diagonally to yield 48 half-square triangles.

From the lengthwise grain of the leaf print, cut in order:

4 strips, 5¾" wide

12 squares, 4" x 4", from the remaining width of fabric

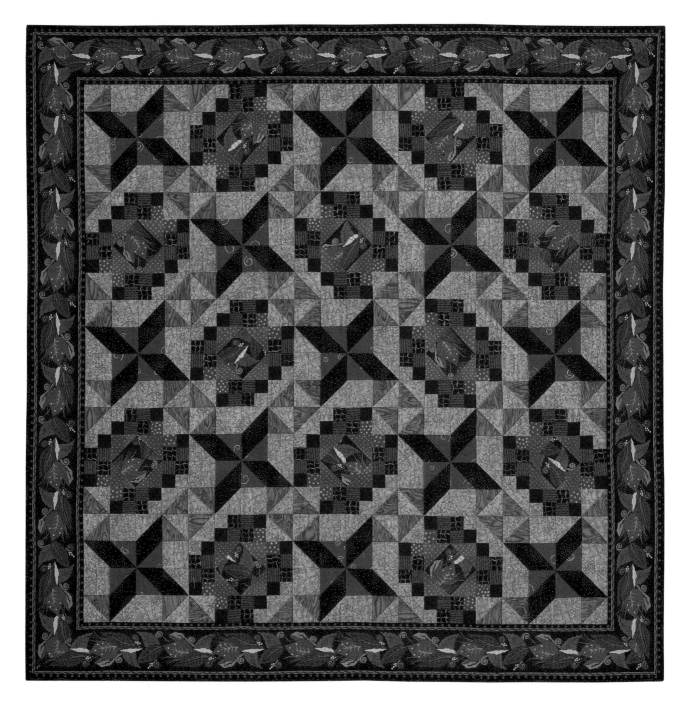

"Connect the Dots" by Nancy Mahoney. I love fabric with dots! Not only were different dot fabrics incorporated into this quilt, but the border also has lines of dots that encircle the edges.

Finished Quilt Size: 61" x 61" ■ *Finished Block Size: 10"*

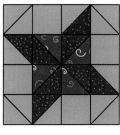

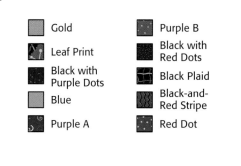

Gold

Leaf Print

Black with Purple Dots

Blue

Purple A

Purple B

Black with Red Dots

Black Plaid

Black-and-Red Stripe

Red Dot

Whirling Pinwheel

Irish Chain

Whirling Pinwheel Blocks

1. Pair each of the 18" x 21" pieces of purple A with an 18" x 21" piece of black with purple dots, right sides facing up. Cut and piece 3"-wide bias strips, following the directions on page 22 for making half-square-triangle units. Make three strip sets. Cut 52 half-square-triangle units, each 3" x 3".

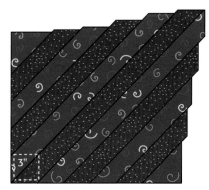

Make 3 strip sets.
Cut 52 units.

2. Pair one 18" x 21" piece of gold with each remaining 18" x 21" piece of black with purple dots, right sides facing up. Cut and piece 3"-wide bias strips, following the directions on page 22 for making half-square-triangle units. Make three strip sets. Cut 52 half-square-triangle units, each 3" x 3".

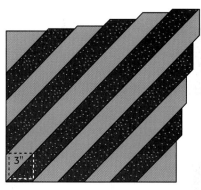

Make 3 strip sets.
Cut 52 units.

3. Pair each remaining 18" x 21" piece of gold with an 18" x 21" piece of blue, right sides facing up. Cut and piece 3"-wide bias strips, following the directions on page 22 for making half-square-triangle units. Make five strip sets. Cut 100 half-square-triangle units, each 3" x 3". You'll use 52 half-square-triangle units for the Whirling Pinwheel blocks and 48 units for the Irish Chain blocks. Set the Irish Chain units aside.

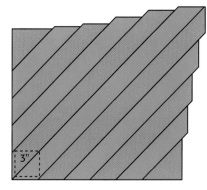

Make 5 strip sets.
Cut 100 units.

4. Join one blue-and-gold half-square-triangle unit, one gold-and-black half-square-triangle unit, one black-and-purple half-square-triangle unit, and one gold 3" square to make a quarter of a Whirling Pinwheel block. Refer to "Pressing Four-Patch Units" on page 22 for tips on pressing the center seams. Make 4 quarter units for each block (52 total).

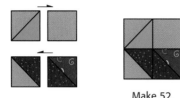

Make 52.

5. Join four of the quarter units to make one Whirling Pinwheel block. Refer to "Pressing Four-Patch Units" on page 22 for tips on pressing the center seams. Make 13 blocks.

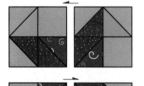

Make 13.

Irish Chain Blocks

1. Referring to "Making Strip Sets" on page 24, join one red dot strip, one black plaid strip, one black-and-red stripe strip, and one black-with-red-dots strip to make strip set A. Repeat to make a total of three. Crosscut the strip sets into 48 segments, each 1¾" wide. Join one black-with-red-dots strip, one black-and-red stripe strip, one black plaid strip, and one gold strip to make strip set B. Repeat to make a total of three. Crosscut the strip sets into 48 segments, each 1¾" wide.

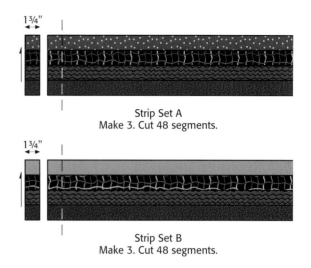

Strip Set A
Make 3. Cut 48 segments.

Strip Set B
Make 3. Cut 48 segments.

2. Join one segment from strip set B to one segment from strip set A to make one side unit. Press. Repeat to make 2 side units for each block (24 total).

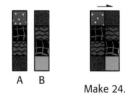

B A

Make 24.

3. Join one segment from strip set A to one segment from strip set B to make one side unit. Press. Repeat to make 2 side units for each block (24 total).

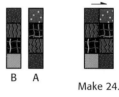

A B

Make 24.

4. Join four purple B 3⅜" triangles to one leaf print 4" square to make one center unit. Press. Make 12.

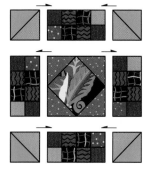

Make 12.

5. Join four blue-and-gold half-square-triangle units, four side units, and one center unit into rows. Press. Join rows to make one Irish Chain block. Press. Make 12 blocks.

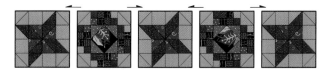

Make 12.

Quilt-Top Assembly

1. Arrange and sew the blocks together in five rows of five blocks each, alternating the Whirling Pinwheel and Irish Chain blocks. Press. Join rows to complete the quilt top. Press.

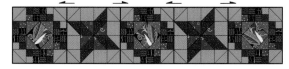

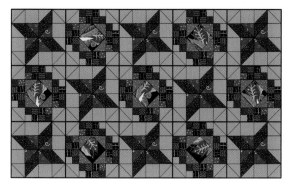

2. Referring to "Borders with Mitered Corners" on pages 26–27, measure and trim the border strips and sew them to the side edges of the quilt top first, and then the top and bottom edges.

Finishing

1. Referring to "Layering the Quilt" on pages 28–29, layer the quilt top with batting and backing. Baste.

2. Referring to "Quilting" on page 29, quilt straight lines across the blocks.

3. Referring to "Squaring Up a Quilt" on page 31, square up the quilt sandwich.

4. Referring to "Binding" on pages 31–32, prepare and sew the binding to the quilt.

Alternate Fabric Plan

Replace several pieces with a lighter background fabric and you have a stunning new secondary design.

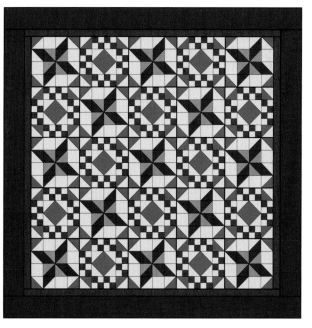

"Stars and Checks"

Connect the Dots

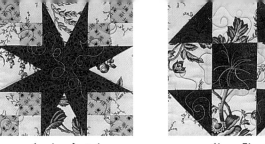

Garden Patch   Shoo Fly

PROVENCE GARDEN

Materials

Yardage is based on 42"-wide fabric.

- 2 yards of blue print for Shoo Fly blocks, outer border, and binding
- 1 yard of background print A for Garden Patch and Shoo Fly blocks
- ¾ yard of background print B for Garden Patch and Shoo Fly blocks
- ⅝ yard of yellow print for Garden Patch blocks and inner border
- 1 fat quarter *each* of 3 blue prints for Garden Patch blocks
- 3 yards of fabric for backing
- 53" x 53" piece of batting

Cutting

All measurements include ¼" seam allowances.

From the yellow print, cut:

9 strips, 1¾" x 42"

From background print B, cut:

5 strips, 1¾" x 42"

2 pieces, 10½" x 21"

From *each* of 2 blue fat quarters, cut:

4 squares, 3" x 3" (8 total)

16 rectangles, 2" x 3¾" (32 total); cut 16 rectangles once diagonally from top left to bottom right to yield 32 triangles and cut 16 rectangles once diagonally from top right to bottom left to yield 32 reverse triangles.

From the remaining blue fat quarter, cut:

5 squares, 3" x 3"

20 rectangles, 2" x 3¾"; cut 10 rectangles once diagonally from top left to bottom right to yield 20 triangles and cut 10 rectangles once diagonally from top right to bottom left to yield 20 reverse triangles.

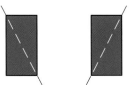

Cut left to right.   Cut right to left.

From background print A, cut:

4 strips, 3" x 42"; crosscut into 48 squares, 3" x 3"

5 strips, 3¼" x 42"; crosscut into 52 squares, 3¼" x 3¼". Cut twice diagonally from center of square side to each corner to yield 52 triangles.

From the 2 yards of blue print, cut in order:

6 strips, 2" x 42", from the crosswise grain

4 strips, 4½" x the remaining lengthwise grain

2 pieces, 10½" x 21", from the remaining width of fabric

12 squares, 3" x 3", from the remaining width of fabric

"Provence Garden" by Nancy Mahoney. Machine quilted by Jan Ogg. The Garden Patch
and Shoo Fly blocks are combined with the colors of Provence, France, to create a wonderful fresh feeling.

Finished Quilt Size: 48½" x 48½" ■ *Finished Block Size: 7½"*

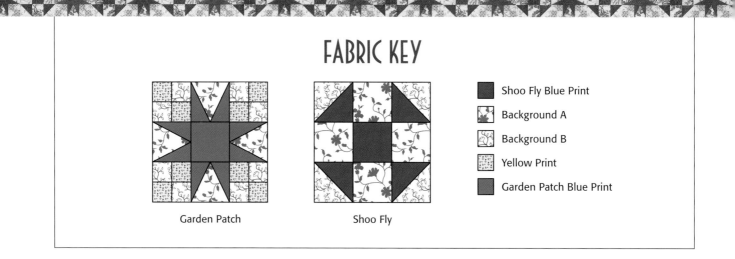

FABRIC KEY

Garden Patch

Shoo Fly

■ Shoo Fly Blue Print
□ Background A
□ Background B
□ Yellow Print
■ Garden Patch Blue Print

Garden Patch Blocks

1. Referring to "Making Strip Sets" on page 24, join one yellow 1¾"-wide strip to one 1¾"-wide background print B strip. Press. Make five strip sets. Cut the strip sets into 104 segments, each 1¾" wide.

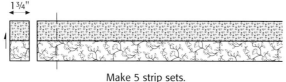

Make 5 strip sets.
Cut 104 segments.

2. Referring to "Pressing Four-Patch Units" on page 22, join two segments to make one four-patch unit. Make 52 units.

Make 52.

3. Join two matching blue triangles to a background print A triangle to make a star-point unit. Press.

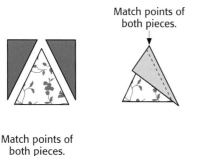

Match points of both pieces.

Match points of both pieces.

Press.

Press.

Trim to 3" x 3".

4. Join 4 four-patch units, four matching star-point units, and one blue 3" square that matches the star-point units into rows. Press. Join rows to make one Garden Patch block. Press. Make 13 blocks.

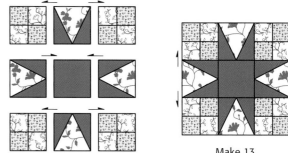

Make 13.

Shoo Fly Blocks

1. Pair each 10½" x 21" piece of background print B with a 10½" x 21" piece of blue print, right sides facing up. Cut and piece 3"-wide bias strips, following the directions on page 22 to make half-square-triangle units. Make four strip sets. Cut 48 half-square-triangle units, each 3" x 3".

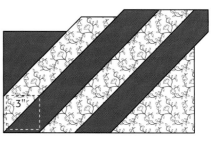

Make 4 strip sets.
Cut 48 units.

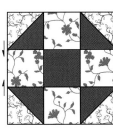

2. Join four half-square-triangle units, four 3" squares from background print A, and one blue print 3" square that matches the half-square-triangle units into rows. Press. Join rows to make one Shoo Fly block. Press. Make 12 blocks.

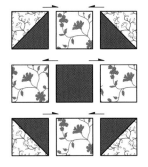

Make 12.

Quilt-Top Assembly

1. Arrange and sew the blocks together in five rows of five blocks each, alternating the Garden Patch and Shoo Fly blocks. Press.

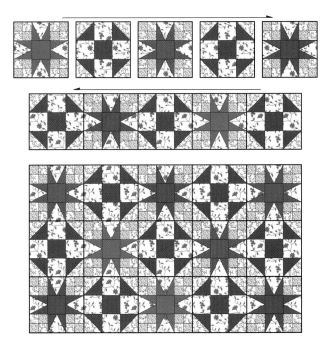

2. Referring to "Borders with Overlapped Corners" on pages 25–26, measure and cut the inner-border strips and sew them to the side edges of the quilt top first, and then to the top and bottom edges. Press. Repeat for the outer border.

Finishing

1. Referring to "Layering the Quilt" on pages 28–29, layer the quilt top with batting and backing. Baste.

2. Referring to "Quilting" on page 29, quilt a design on the diagonal on top of the Garden Patch blocks and a motif over the Shoo Fly blocks.

3. Referring to "Squaring Up a Quilt" on page 31, square up the quilt sandwich.

4. Referring to "Binding" on pages 31–32, prepare and sew the binding to the quilt.

Alternate Fabric Plan

The Shoo Fly blocks recede with the change to a darker value background, and a circular pattern similar to a Pickle Dish emerges.

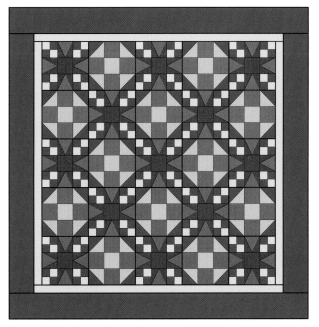

"Pickled Stars"

Windmill   **Around the Square**

FIESTA

Materials

Yardage is based on 42"-wide fabric.

- 2½ yards of black print for Windmill and Around the Square blocks, border, and binding
- ⅞ yard of purple print for Around the Square and Windmill blocks
- ⅝ yard of red print for Windmill blocks
- ⅝ yard of yellow print for Windmill blocks
- ⅝ yard of orange print for Around the Square and Windmill blocks
- ⅜ yard of green print for Around the Square blocks
- 3¼ yards of fabric for backing
- 54" x 54" piece of batting

Cutting

All measurements include ¼" seam allowances.

From the red print, cut:

2 pieces, 18" x 21"

From the yellow print, cut:

2 pieces, 18" x 21"

From the orange print, cut:

1 piece, 18" x 21"

24 squares, 2⅞" x 2⅞"; cut once diagonally to yield 48 triangles

From the purple print, cut:

6 strips, 2½" x 42"; crosscut into 48 rectangles, 2½" x 4½"

1 piece, 18" x 21"

From the black print, cut in order:

1 strip, 3⅜" x 42", from the crosswise grain; crosscut into 12 squares, 3⅜" x 3⅜"

6 strips, 2" x 42", from the crosswise grain

4 strips, 5" x the remaining lengthwise grain

52 squares, 2⅞" x 2⅞", from the remaining width of fabric; cut each square once diagonally to yield 104 half-square triangles

96 squares, 2½" x 2½", from the remaining width of fabric

From the green print, cut:

3 strips, 2½" x 42"; crosscut into 48 squares, 2½" x 2½"

"Fiesta" by Nancy Mahoney. Machine quilted by Jan Ogg. The fabric placement creates
an exciting overall design that results in a visual puzzle.

Finished Quilt Size: 49½" x 49½" ■ *Finished Block Size: 8"*

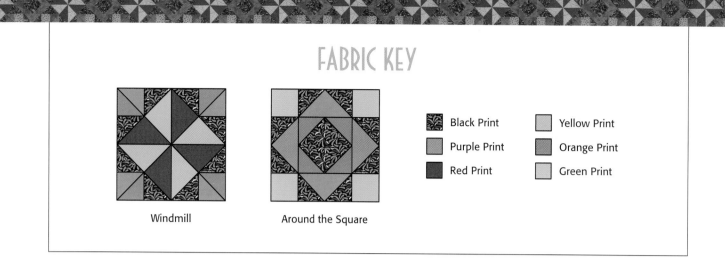

FABRIC KEY

Windmill

Around the Square

- Black Print
- Purple Print
- Red Print
- Yellow Print
- Orange Print
- Green Print

Windmill Blocks

1. Pair each 18" x 21" piece of red print with an 18" x 21" piece of yellow print, right sides facing up. Cut and piece 3¼"-wide bias strips, following the directions on page 22 for making half-square-triangle units. Make four strip sets. Cut 52 half-square-triangle units, each 3⅜" x 3⅜".

Make 4 strip sets.
Cut 52 units.

2. Pair an 18" x 21" piece of orange print with an 18" x 21" piece of purple print, right sides facing up. Cut and piece 2½"-wide bias strips, following the directions on page 22 for making half-square-triangle units. Make two strip sets. Cut 52 half-square-triangle units, each 2½" x 2½".

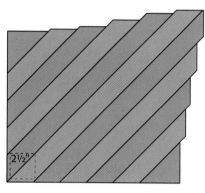

Make 2 strip sets.
Cut 52 units.

3. Join two black 2⅞" triangles to one orange-and-purple half-square-triangle unit to make one corner unit. Press. Make 4 corner units for each block (52 total).

Make 52.

4. Join four red-and-yellow half-square-triangle units to make one center unit. Refer to "Pressing Four-Patch Units" on page 22 for tips on pressing the center seams. Make 1 center unit for each block (13 total).

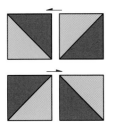
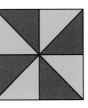

Make 13.

5. Join four corner units and one center unit to make one Windmill block. Press. Make 13 blocks.

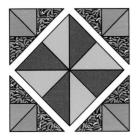

Make 13.

Around the Square Blocks

1. Referring to the directions on page 24 for making flying-geese units, join two black 2½" squares to one purple rectangle to make one side unit. Press. Make 4 for each block (48 total).

Make 48.

2. Join four orange 2⅞" triangles to one black 3⅜" square to make one center unit. Press. Make 1 for each block (12 total).

Make 12.

3. Join four green 2½" squares, four side units, and one center unit into rows. Press. Join rows to make one Around the Square block. Press. Make 12 blocks.

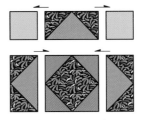
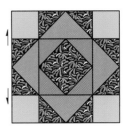

Make 12.

Quilt-Top Assembly

1. Arrange and sew the blocks together in five rows of five blocks each, alternating the Windmill blocks and Around the Square blocks. Press.

2. Referring to "Borders with Overlapped Corners" on pages 25–26, measure and cut the 5"-wide border strips and sew them to the side edges of the quilt top first, and then to the top and bottom edges. Press.

Finishing

1. Referring to "Layering the Quilt" on pages 28–29, layer the quilt top with batting and backing. Baste.
2. Referring to "Quilting" on page 29, quilt circles across the center.
3. Referring to "Squaring Up a Quilt" on page 31, square up the quilt sandwich.
4. Referring to "Binding" on pages 31–32, prepare and sew the binding to the quilt.

Alternate Fabric Plan

By adding a light background, the pinwheels disappear and a different secondary design emerges.

"Melrose Stars"

Favorite Star

Stepping Stones

SIROCCO

Materials

Yardage is based on 42"-wide fabric.

- 3⅜ yards of navy mottled batik for Favorite Star and Stepping Stones blocks and border
- 1⅝ yards of red-and-navy batik print for Favorite Star and Stepping Stones blocks
- ⅞ yard of yellow solid batik for Favorite Star blocks
- ¾ yard of cream solid batik for Favorite Star and Stepping Stones blocks
- ¾ yard of navy leaf batik print for Favorite Star and Stepping Stones blocks
- ⅝ yard of yellow leaf batik print for Favorite Star blocks
- ⅝ yard of gold mottled batik print for Stepping Stones blocks
- ¼ yard of brick dot batik print for Favorite Star blocks
- ¼ yard of yellow stripe batik print for Favorite Star blocks
- 4½ yards of fabric for backing
- ⅝ yard of dark navy solid batik for binding
- 75" x 75" piece of batting

Cutting

All measurements include ¼" seam allowances.

From the yellow solid batik, cut:

2 strips, 2⅜" x 42"; crosscut into 20 squares, 2⅜" x 2⅜". Cut each square once diagonally to yield 40 half-square triangles.

5 squares, 10" x 10"

From the yellow leaf batik print, cut:

2 strips, 2⅜" x 42"; crosscut into 20 squares, 2⅜" x 2⅜". Cut each square once diagonally to yield 40 half-square triangles.

2 squares, 10" x 10"

From the navy mottled batik, cut in order:

9 strips, 2" x 42", from the crosswise grain

1 strip, 10" x 42", from the crosswise grain; crosscut into 4 squares, 10" x 10"

2 strips, 3½" x 42", from the crosswise grain; crosscut 1 of the strips into 20 rectangles, 2" x 3½"

4 strips, 5½" x the remaining lengthwise grain

48 pieces with template A (page 63) from the remaining width of fabric

104 squares, 2" x 2", from the remaining width of fabric

3 squares, 10" x 10", from the remaining width of fabric

From the red-and-navy batik print, cut:

3 strips, 3⅞" x 42"; crosscut into 26 squares, 3⅞" x 3⅞". Cut each square once diagonally to yield 52 half-square triangles.

20 strips, 2" x 42"; crosscut 5 strips into 52 rectangles, 2" x 3½'

From the yellow stripe batik print, cut:

2 strips, 2⅜" x 42"; crosscut into 12 squares, 2⅜" x 2⅜". Cut each square once diagonally to yield 24 half-square triangles.

(Continued on page 59)

"Sirocco" by Nancy Mahoney. Machine quilted by Barbara Dau. Favorite Star and Stepping Stones blocks are combined with batik fabrics to create a fabulous design. The blocks appear to float on top of the border.

Finished Quilt Size: 70½" x 70½" ■ *Finished Block Size: 12"*

FABRIC KEY

Favorite Star

Stepping Stones

Fabric Key:
- Navy Mottled Batik
- Red and Navy Batik
- Yellow Solid Batik
- Cream Solid Batik
- Navy Leaf Batik
- Yellow Leaf Batik
- Gold Mottled Batik
- Brick Dot Batik
- Yellow Stripe Batik

(Continued from page 57)

From the brick dot batik print, cut:

3 strips, 2" x 42"; crosscut into 52 squares, 2" x 2"

From the cream solid batik, cut:

4 strips, 2" x 42"

4 strips, 3½" x 42"; crosscut 2 of the strips into 32 rectangles, 2" x 3½"

From the navy leaf batik print, cut:

3 strips, 3½" x 42"; crosscut into 25 squares, 3½" x 3½"

48 pieces with template A on page 63

From the gold mottled batik print, cut:

96 pieces with template B on page 63

From the dark navy solid batik, cut:

8 strips, 2" x 42"

Favorite Star Blocks

1. Pair each 10" square of yellow solid and yellow leaf batik with a 10" square of navy mottled batik, right sides facing up. Cut and piece 3¾"-wide bias strips, following the directions on page 22 for making half-square-triangle units. Make a total of 13 strip sets. Cut 3⅞" half-square-triangle units from each strip set. You will need 4 matching half-square-triangle units for each block (52 units total).

Make 9 strip sets.
Cut 36 units.

Make 4 strip sets.
Cut 16 units.

2. Referring to "Quarter-Square-Triangle Units" on page 24, crosscut each half-square-triangle unit on the diagonal to yield two quarter-square-triangle units.

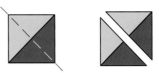

3. Sew two matching quarter-square-triangle units together. Refer to "Pressing Four-Patch Units" on page 22 for pressing the center seam. Make a total of 52 units—36 with yellow solid and 16 with yellow leaf.

Make 36.   Make 16.

NOTE: Make this unit with two quarter-square-triangle units from either the right or the left side of the diagonal cut. Turn one quarter-square-triangle unit so that the navy triangles oppose each other as shown.

4. Referring to the directions on page 24 for making flying-geese units, join two navy mottled batik 2" squares to one red-and-navy rectangle to make one unit. Press. Make 52.

Make 52.

5. Join a unit from step 3 to a flying-geese unit to make one side unit. Press. Make 4 matching side units for each block (52 total).

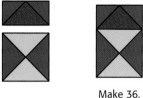

Make 36.   Make 16.

6. Join two yellow 2⅜" triangles to one brick dot square to make a unit. Press. Make 20 units with the yellow solid triangles, 20 units with the yellow leaf print, and 12 units with the yellow stripe.

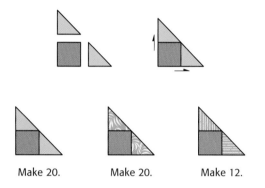

Make 20.   Make 20.   Make 12.

7. Join one red-and-navy 3⅞" triangle to each unit from step 6 to make a corner unit. Press. Make 52 corner units.

Make 20.   Make 20.   Make 12.

8. Refer to "Making Strip Sets" on page 24. Join each cream batik 3½"-wide strip to one red-and-navy 2"-wide strip. Press. Make two strip sets and cross-cut them into 32 segments, each 2" wide. Join one navy mottled batik 3½"-wide strip to one red-and-navy 2"-wide strip. Press. Crosscut the strip set into 20 segments, each 2" wide.

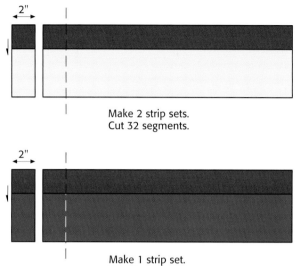

Make 2 strip sets.
Cut 32 segments.

Make 1 strip set.
Cut 20 segments.

9. Join a 3½" rectangle (cream solid or navy mottled) to one side of the corner unit from step 7; then join a 2"-wide segment from step 8 to make a complete corner unit. Refer to the illustrations below for color placement and unit quantities.

 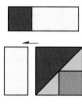

Make 20.

Make 12.   Make 20.

10. Join four corner units, four side units, and one navy leaf batik print square into rows. Press. Join rows to make one Favorite Star block. Press. Refer to the illustrations below for color placement and block quantities.

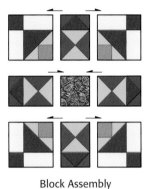

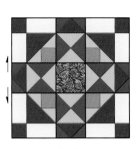

Block Assembly

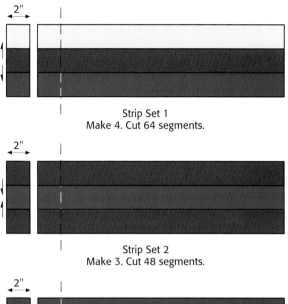

Block A
Make 5.

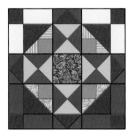

Block B
Make 4.

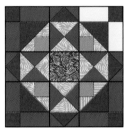

Block C
Make 4.

Stepping Stones Blocks

1. Referring to "Making Strip Sets" on page 24, join 2" x 42" strips of cream solid batik, red-and-navy batik, and navy mottled batik in groups of three to make strip sets 1, 2, and 3. Crosscut the strip sets into 2"-wide segments as indicated.

Strip Set 1
Make 4. Cut 64 segments.

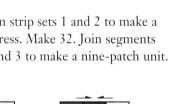

Strip Set 2
Make 3. Cut 48 segments.

Strip Set 3
Make 2. Cut 32 segments.

2. Join segments from strip sets 1 and 2 to make a nine-patch unit. Press. Make 32. Join segments from strip sets 2 and 3 to make a nine-patch unit. Press. Make 16.

Make 32.

Make 16.

3. Join one navy leaf piece cut with template A to one gold batik piece cut with template B. Join one navy mottled batik piece cut with template A to one gold batik piece cut with template B. Press. Join the two pieces to make a rectangle unit. Press. Make 4 rectangle units for each block (48 total).

Make 48.

4. Join four nine-patch units, four rectangle units, and one navy leaf batik print square into rows. Press. Join rows to make a Stepping Stones block. Press. Refer to the illustrations below for color placement and block quantities.

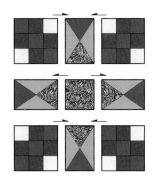

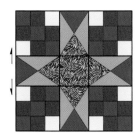

Block D
Make 4.

Block E
Make 8.

Quilt-Top Assembly

1. Arrange the Favorite Star and Stepping Stones blocks as shown and sew the blocks together in five rows of five blocks each. Press.

2. Referring to "Borders with Overlapped Corners" on pages 25–26, measure and cut the border strips and sew them to the side edges of the quilt top first, and then to the top and bottom edges. Press.

Finishing

1. Referring to "Layering the Quilt" on pages 28–29, layer the quilt top with batting and backing. Baste.

2. Referring to "Quilting" on page 29, quilt all the blocks in the ditch. Quilt a motif in the center star of the Stepping Stones blocks and on top of the chain of squares. Also quilt a feather motif in the border.

3. Referring to "Squaring Up a Quilt" on page 31, square up the quilt sandwich.

4. Referring to "Binding" on pages 31–32, prepare and sew the binding to the quilt.

Alternate Fabric Plan

The addition of more background areas makes a subtle but exciting new focus on the secondary design.

"Kenta"

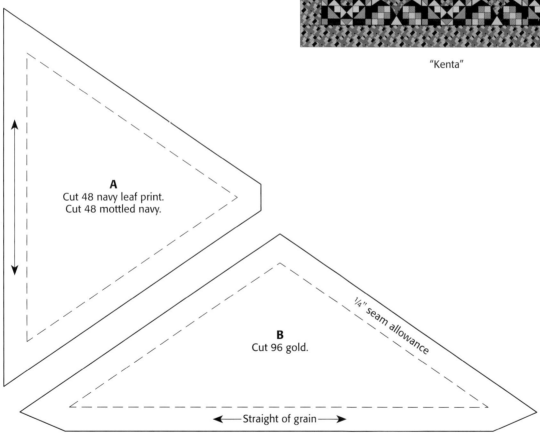

A
Cut 48 navy leaf print.
Cut 48 mottled navy.

B
Cut 96 gold.

¼" seam allowance

← Straight of grain →

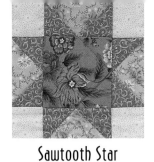 

Sawtooth Star   Mosaic

SUNDANCE

Materials

Yardage is based on 42"-wide fabric.

- 1⅛ yards of olive green floral print for Mosaic blocks, outer border, and binding
- ⅞ yard of beige print for Sawtooth Star blocks, Mosaic blocks, and inner border
- ¾ yard of gold print for Sawtooth Star blocks and inner border
- ⅜ yard of tan floral print for Sawtooth Star blocks
- ¼ yard of red print for Mosaic blocks
- ¼ yard of dark green print for Mosaic blocks
- ¼ yard of cream print for Sawtooth Star blocks
- 2½ yards of fabric for backing (If the backing fabric is wide enough, 1¼ yards of fabric may be enough.)
- 45" x 45" piece of batting

Cutting

All measurements include ¼" seam allowances.

From the gold print, cut:

6 strips, 2" x 42"; crosscut into 120 squares, 2" x 2"

3 strips, 2" x 42"; crosscut into four 2" x 8" rectangles and eight 2" x 9½" rectangles

From the beige print, cut:

6 strips, 2" x 42"; crosscut into 60 rectangles, 2" x 3½"

48 pieces with template (page 68)

From the cream print, cut:

3 strips, 2" x 42"; crosscut into 52 squares, 2" x 2"

From the tan floral print, cut:

2 strips, 3½" x 42"; crosscut into 13 squares, 3½" x 3½"

From the olive green floral print, cut:

2 strips, 3½" x 42"; crosscut into 12 squares, 3½" x 3½"

5 strips, 2" x 42"

4 strips, 4" x 42"

From the red print, cut:

2 strips, 3" x 42"; crosscut into 24 squares, 3" x 3". Cut each square once diagonally to yield 48 half-square triangles.

From the dark green print, cut:

2 strips, 2⅜" x 42"; crosscut into 24 squares, 2⅜" x 2⅜". Cut each square once diagonally to yield 48 half-square triangles.

"Sundance" by Nancy Mahoney. The Sawtooth Star blocks take a backseat to the strong graphics of the Mosaic blocks, which are further enhanced by their extensions into the inner border.

Finished Quilt Size: 40½" x 40½" ■ *Finished Block Size: 6"*

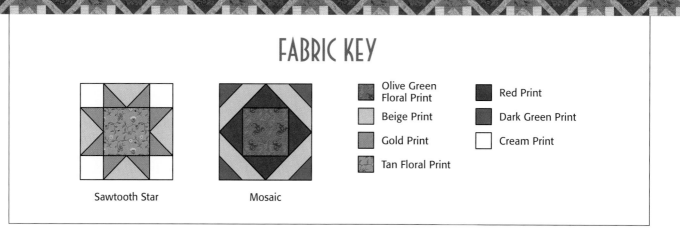

FABRIC KEY

Sawtooth Star

Mosaic

- Olive Green Floral Print
- Beige Print
- Gold Print
- Tan Floral Print
- Red Print
- Dark Green Print
- Cream Print

Sawtooth Star Blocks

1. Referring to the directions on page 24 for making flying-geese units, join two gold 2" squares to one beige rectangle to make one side unit. Press. Make 4 side units for each block (52 total).

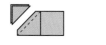

Make 52.

2. Join four cream 2" squares, four flying-geese units, and one tan floral 3½" square into rows. Press. Join rows to make one Sawtooth Star block. Press. Make 13 blocks.

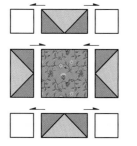
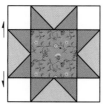

Make 13.

Mosaic Blocks

1. Join four red 3" triangles to one olive green floral 3½" square to make one center unit. Press. Make 12.

Make 12.

2. Join four beige pieces cut with template (page 68) to the center unit. Press. Make 12.

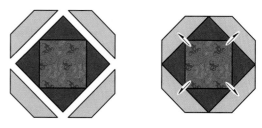

3. Join four dark green 2⅜" triangles to a center unit to make one Mosaic block. Press. Make 12.

Make 12.

Quilt-Top Assembly

1. Arrange and sew the blocks together in five rows of five blocks each, alternating the Sawtooth Star and Mosaic blocks. Press.

NOTE: The quilt top must measure 30½" x 30½" at this point for the pieced border to fit properly.

2. For the inner-border strips, refer to "Making Flying-Geese Units" on page 24. Join two gold print 2" squares to one beige 2" x 3½" rectangle to make one unit. Press. Make eight units.

Make 8.

3. Join two gold 2" x 8" rectangles, one gold 2" x 9½" rectangle, and two flying-geese units to make one side inner border. Press. Repeat.

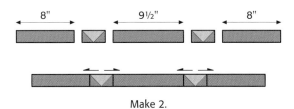

Make 2.

4. Join three gold 2" x 9½" rectangles and two flying-geese units to make one top inner-border strip. Press. Repeat for the bottom inner-border strip.

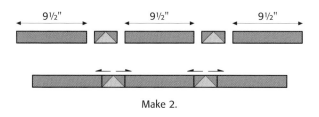

Make 2.

5. Referring to "Borders with Overlapped Corners" on pages 25–26, sew the inner-border strips to the side edges of the quilt top first, and then to the top and bottom edges. Press. Be careful to match the seams of the flying-geese units with the block seams to ensure the continuity of the block design.

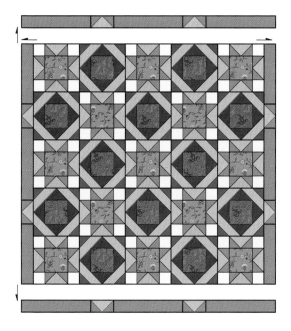

6. Referring to "Borders with Overlapped Corners" on pages 25–26, measure and cut the 4"-wide outer-border strips. Sew them to the side edges of the quilt top first, and then to the top and bottom edges. Press.

Finishing

1. Referring to "Layering the Quilt" on pages 28–29, layer the quilt top with batting and backing. Baste.

2. Referring to "Quilting" on page 29, quilt straight lines on the diagonal in both directions.

3. Referring to "Squaring Up a Quilt" on page 31, square up the quilt sandwich.

4. Referring to "Binding" on pages 31–32, prepare and sew the binding to the quilt.

Alternate Fabric Plan

Moving the darkest value to the Sawtooth Stars blocks creates a new focus in the quilt design.

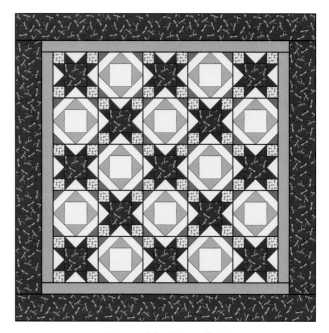

"Dance of the Dragonflies"

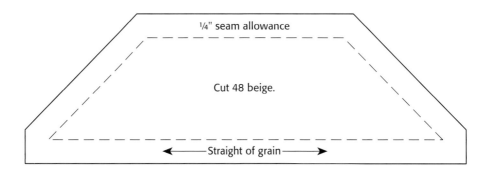

¼" seam allowance

Cut 48 beige.

←——— Straight of grain ———→

Queen's Crown

'Round the Corner

Queen's Crossing

Materials

Yardage is based on 42"-wide fabric.

- 2¼ yards of large floral print for border
- 2⅛ yards of tan print A for Queen's Crown blocks
- 1½ yards of cream print for 'Round the Corner blocks
- 1⅜ yards of red print A for 'Round the Corner blocks
- 1⅛ yards of medium floral print for Queen's Crown blocks
- 1⅛ yards of red print B for Queen's Crown blocks
- ⅝ yard of moss green print for Queen's Crown blocks
- ½ yard of tan print B for Queen's Crown blocks
- 4⅜ yards of fabric for backing
- ⅝ yard of fabric for binding
- 76" x 76" piece of batting

Cutting

All measurements include ¼" seam allowances.

From the tan print A, cut:

8 pieces, 18" x 21"

From the moss green print, cut:

2 pieces, 18" x 21"

From red print B, cut:

7 strips, 2½" x 42"; crosscut into 100 squares, 2½" x 2½"

2 pieces, 18" x 21"

From the medium floral print, cut:

4 pieces, 18" x 21"

From the tan print B, cut:

5 strips, 2½" x 42"; crosscut into 80 squares, 2½" x 2½"

From the cream print, cut:

12 strips, 2½" x 42"

2 pieces, 18" x 21"

From red print A, cut:

9 strips, 2½" x 42"

2 pieces, 18" x 21"

From the lengthwise grain of the large floral print, cut:

4 strips, 6" wide

From the binding fabric, cut:

8 strips, 2" x 42"

"Queen's Crossing" by Julie Sheckman, Blue Bell, Pennsylvania. A unique secondary pattern is formed when the two blocks—Queen's Crown and 'Round the Corner—are combined.

Finished Quilt Size: 71½" x 71½" ■ *Finished Block Size: 10"*

FABRIC KEY

Queen's Crown

'Round the Corner

- Tan Print A
- Cream Print
- Red Print A
- Medium Floral
- Red Print B
- Moss Green Print
- Tan Print B

Queen's Crown Blocks

1. Pair an 18" x 21" piece of tan print A with each 18" x 21" piece of moss green print, right sides facing up. Cut and piece 2½"-wide bias strips, following the directions on page 22 for making half-square-triangle units. Make four strip sets. Cut 80 half-square-triangle units, each 2½" x 2½".

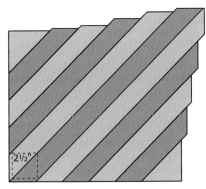

Make 4 strip sets.
Cut 80 units.

2. Pair an 18" x 21" piece of tan print A with each 18" x 21" piece of red print B, right sides facing up. Cut and piece 2½"-wide bias strips, following the directions on page 22 for making half-square-triangle units. Make four strip sets. Cut 80 half-square-triangle units, each 2½" x 2½".

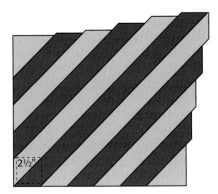

Make 4 strip sets.
Cut 80 units.

3. Pair an 18" x 21" piece of tan print A with each 18" x 21" piece of medium floral print, right sides facing up. Cut and piece 2½"-wide bias strips, following the directions on page 22 for making half-square-triangle units. Make eight strip sets. Cut 160 half-square-triangle units, each 2½" x 2½".

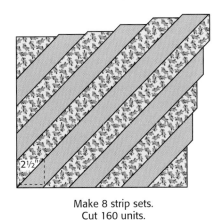

Make 8 strip sets.
Cut 160 units.

4. Join two red print B 2½" squares and two tan-print-A-and-moss-green half-square-triangle units to make a corner unit. Press. Make 2 matching corner units for each block (40 total).

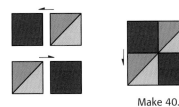

Make 40.

5. Join two tan print B 2½" squares and two tan-print-A-and-floral half-square-triangle units to make a corner unit. Press. Make 2 matching corner units for each block (40 total).

Make 40.

6. Join one tan-print-A-and-red half-square-triangle unit and one tan-print-A-and-floral half-square-triangle unit to make a side unit. Make 2 side units (40 total) and 2 reversed side units (40 total) for each block. Press.

Make 40.

Make 40.

7. Join two red corner units, two tan corner units, one 2½" red square, two side units, and two reversed side units into rows. Press. Join rows to make one Queen's Crown block. Press. Make 20 blocks.

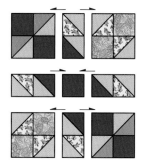
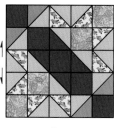

Make 20.

'Round the Corner Blocks

1. Pair an 18" x 21" piece of cream print with each 18" x 21" piece of red print A, right sides facing up. Cut and piece 2½"-wide bias strips, following the directions on page 22 for making half-square-triangle units. Make four strip sets. Cut 64 half-square-triangle units, each 2½" x 2½".

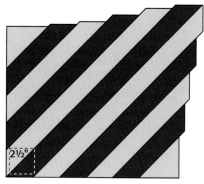

2½"

Make 4 strip sets.
Cut 64 units.

2. Referring to "Making Strip Sets" on page 24, join two cream print strips to one red print A strip to make strip set A. Make two total. Join three cream print strips and two red print A strips to make strip set B. Make two total. Join three red print A strips and two cream print strips to make one strip set C. Press. Crosscut the strip set As into 32 segments, each 2½" wide. Crosscut the strip set Bs into 32 segments, each 2½" wide. And crosscut strip set C into 16 segments, each 2½" wide.

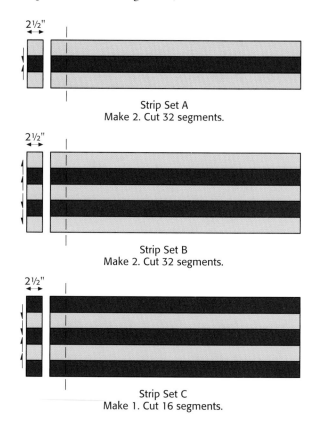

2½"

Strip Set A
Make 2. Cut 32 segments.

2½"

Strip Set B
Make 2. Cut 32 segments.

2½"

Strip Set C
Make 1. Cut 16 segments.

3. Arrange four half-square-triangle units, two strip set A segments, two strip set B segments, and one strip set C segment into rows. Press. Join rows to make one 'Round the Corner block. Press. Make 16 blocks.

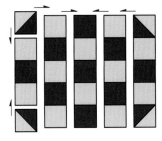 

Make 16.

Quilt-Top Assembly

1. Arrange the Queen's Crown and 'Round the Corner blocks as shown and sew the blocks together in six rows of six blocks each. Press.

2. Referring to "Borders with Overlapped Corners" on pages 25–26, measure and cut the border strips and sew them to the side edges of the quilt top first, and then to the top and bottom edges. Press.

Finishing

1. Referring to "Layering the Quilt" on pages 28–29, layer the quilt top with batting and backing. Baste.

2. Referring to "Quilting" on page 29, quilt with an allover stipple pattern.

3. Referring to "Squaring Up a Quilt" on page 31, square up the quilt sandwich.

4. Referring to "Binding" on pages 31–32, prepare and sew the binding to the quilt.

Alternate Fabric Plan

By changing the position of the darkest value and using only one background fabric, you can achieve a different secondary design.

"Greenbriar"

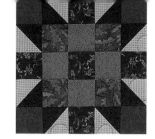
New England

'Round the Corner

MULBERRY ROAD

Materials

Yardage is based on 42"-wide fabric.

- 3 yards of medium purple floral print for 'Round the Corner blocks, New England blocks, and border
- 1⅛ yards of dark purple print A for New England blocks and binding
- 1⅛ yards of tan print for 'Round the Corner and New England blocks
- ¾ yard of red print for 'Round the Corner and New England blocks
- ¾ yard of gold print for 'Round the Corner and New England blocks
- ⅜ yard of leaf print for New England blocks
- 1 fat quarter of dark purple print B for 'Round the Corner blocks
- 4 yards of fabric for backing
- 64" x 64" piece of batting

Cutting

All measurements include ¼" seam allowances.

From the tan print, cut:

3 pieces, 18" x 21"

From dark purple print A, cut:

7 strips, 2" x 42"

2 pieces, 18" x 21"

From the leaf print, cut:

4 strips, 2½" x 42"

From the gold print, cut:

9 strips, 2½" x 42"

From the medium purple floral print, cut in order:

15 strips, 2½" x 42", from the crosswise grain

4 strips, 5" x the remaining lengthwise grain

26 squares, 2½" x 2½", from the remaining width of fabric

From the red print, cut:

8 strips, 2½" x 42"; crosscut 4 strips into 52 squares, 2½" x 2½"

"Mulberry Road" by Nancy Mahoney. Machine quilted by Jan Ogg. The New England blocks and 'Round the Corner blocks blend together beautifully to create an effect reminiscent of a vintage quilt.

Finished Quilt Size: 59½" x 59½" ■ *Finished Block Size: 10"*

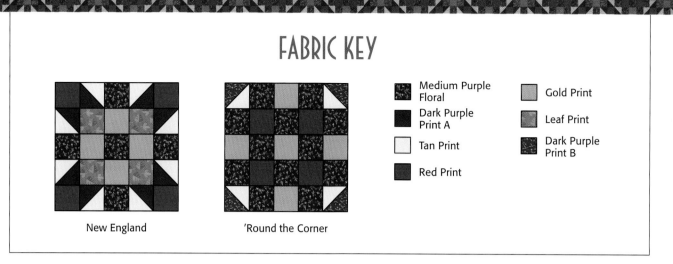

FABRIC KEY

New England

'Round the Corner

Medium Purple Floral

Dark Purple Print A

Tan Print

Red Print

Gold Print

Leaf Print

Dark Purple Print B

New England Blocks

1. Pair an 18" x 21" piece of tan print with each 18" x 21" piece of dark purple print A, right sides facing up. Cut and piece 2½"-wide bias strips, following the directions on page 22 for making half-square-triangle units. Make four strip sets. Cut 104 half-square-triangle units, each 2½" x 2½".

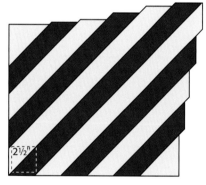

Make 4 strip sets.
Cut 104 units.

2. Referring to "Making Strip Sets" on page 24, join two leaf print strips to one gold strip to make strip set A. Make two total. Join three purple floral 2½" x 42" strips and two gold strips to make one strip set B. Press. Crosscut the strip set As into 26 segments, each 2½" wide. Crosscut strip set B into 13 segments, each 2½" wide.

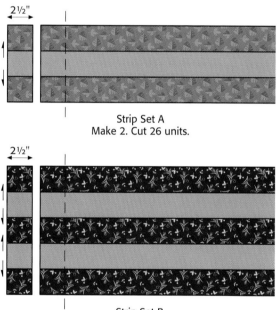

2½"

Strip Set A
Make 2. Cut 26 units.

2½"

Strip Set B
Make 1. Cut 13 units.

3. Join eight half-square-triangle units, two segments from strip set A, one segment from strip set B, four red 2½" squares, and four purple floral squares into rows. Press. Join the rows to make one New England block. Press. Make 13 blocks.

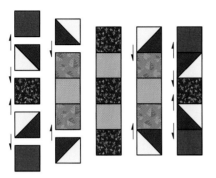

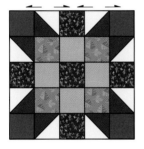

Make 13.

'Round the Corner Blocks

1. Pair an 18" x 21" piece of tan print with the fat quarter of dark purple print B, right sides facing up. Cut and piece 2½"-wide bias strips, following the directions on page 22 for making half-square-triangle units. Make two strip sets. Cut 52 half-square-triangle units, each 2½" x 2½".

Make 2 strip sets.
Cut 52 units.

2. Referring to "Making Strip Sets" on page 24, join two purple floral 2½" x 42" strips to one gold strip to make strip set A. Make two total. Join three purple floral 2½" x 42" strips and two red strips to make strip set B. Make two total. Join three gold strips and two purple floral 2½" x 42" strips to make one strip set C. Crosscut the strip set As into 24 segments, each 2½" wide. Crosscut the strip set Bs into 24 segments, each 2½" wide. Crosscut strip set C into 12 segments, 2½" wide.

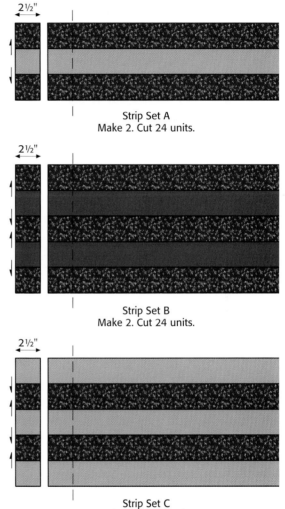

2½"

Strip Set A
Make 2. Cut 24 units.

2½"

Strip Set B
Make 2. Cut 24 units.

2½"

Strip Set C
Make 1. Cut 12 units.

3. Join four half-square-triangle units, two strip set A segments, two strip set B segments, and one strip set C segment to make one 'Round the Corner block. Make 12 blocks.

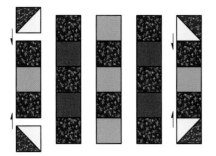

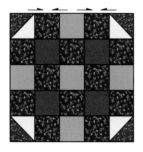

Make 12.

Quilt-Top Assembly

1. Arrange and sew the blocks together in five rows of five blocks each, alternating the New England blocks and 'Round the Corner blocks. Press.

2. Referring to "Borders with Overlapped Corners" on pages 25–26, measure and cut the border strips and sew them to the side edges of the quilt top first, and then the top and bottom edges. Press.

Finishing

1. Referring to "Layering the Quilt" on pages 28–29, layer the quilt top with batting and backing. Baste.

2. Referring to "Quilting" on page 29, quilt feathered wreaths in the 'Round the Corner blocks and quilt the New England blocks in the ditch. Quilt a feather motif in the border.

3. Referring to "Squaring Up a Quilt" on page 31, square up the quilt sandwich.

4. Referring to "Binding" on pages 31–32, prepare and sew the binding to the quilt.

Alternate Fabric Plan

With the addition of more background fabric, stars emerge from the overall design.

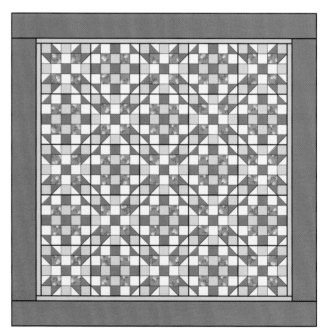

"Purple Passion"

Hovering Hawks

King's Crown

MARBLE MANIA

Materials

Yardage is based on 42"-wide fabric.

- 2⅞ yards of black dot print for Hovering Hawks blocks, border, and binding
- 2⅝ yards of yellow print for Hovering Hawks and King's Crown blocks
- 2⅛ yards of rust dot print for Hovering Hawks and King's Crown blocks
- 1 yard of geometric print for Hovering Hawks and King's Crown blocks
- ⅝ yard of stripe for Hovering Hawks blocks
- ½ yard of purple print for Hovering Hawks blocks
- 4½ yards of fabric for backing
- 75" x 75" piece of batting

Cutting

All measurements include ¼" seam allowances.

From the yellow print, cut:

4 strips, 3⅜" x 42"; crosscut into 40 squares, 3⅜" x 3⅜". Cut each square once diagonally to yield 80 half-square triangles.

18 strips, 3" x 42"; crosscut 8 strips into 104 squares, 3" x 3". Crosscut 10 strips into 64 rectangles, 3" x 5½".

1 piece, 18" x 21"

From the rust dot print, cut:

10 strips, 3" x 42"; crosscut into 128 squares, 3" x 3"

3 pieces, 18" x 21"

From the stripe, cut:

2 pieces, 18" x 21"

From the black dot print, cut in order:

8 strips, 2" x 42", from the crosswise grain

4 strips, 5½" x the remaining lengthwise grain

8 squares, 5⅞" x 5⅞", from the remaining width of fabric; cut each square once diagonally to yield 16 half-square triangles

From the geometric print, cut:

3 strips, 5½" x 42"; crosscut into 16 squares, 5½" x 5½"

2 strips, 5⅞" x 42"; crosscut into 12 squares, 5⅞" x 5⅞". Cut each square once diagonally to yield 24 half-square triangles.

From the purple print, cut:

4 strips, 3" x 42"; crosscut into 40 squares, 3" x 3"

"Marble Mania" by Nancy Mahoney. Machine quilted by Susan Powell.
The exciting secondary design created with the combination of the Hovering Hawks
and King's Crown blocks produces a feeling of motion and great visual interest.

Finished Quilt Size: 70½" x 70½" ■ *Finished Block Size: 10"*

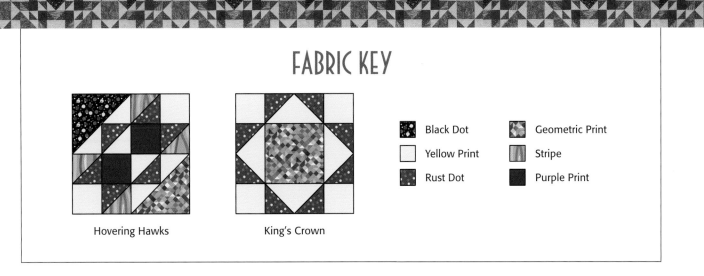

FABRIC KEY

Hovering Hawks

King's Crown

- Black Dot
- Yellow Print
- Rust Dot
- Geometric Print
- Stripe
- Purple Print

Hovering Hawks Blocks

1. Pair the 18" x 21" piece of yellow print with an 18" x 21" piece of rust dot print, right sides facing up. Cut and piece 3"-wide bias strips, following the directions on page 22 for making half-square-triangle units. Make two strip sets. Cut 40 half-square-triangle units, each 3" x 3".

Make 2 strip sets.
Cut 40 units.

2. Pair each 18" x 21" piece of stripe print with an 18" x 21" piece of rust dot print, right sides facing up. Cut and piece 3"-wide bias strips, following the directions on page 22 for making half-square-triangle units. Make four strip sets. Cut 80 half-square-triangle units, each 3" x 3".

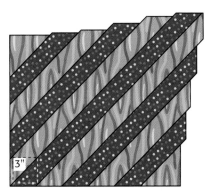

Make 4 strip sets.
Cut 80 units.

3. Join two yellow 3⅜" triangles and one yellow-and-rust-dot half-square-triangle unit to make a unit. Press. Make 2 units for each block (40 total).

Make 40.

4. Join black dot triangles to the units from step 3 to make 16 corner units. Press. Join geometric print triangles to the units from step 3 to make 24 corner units.

Make 16.

Make 24.

5. Join two stripe-and-rust-dot half-square-triangle units, one purple square, and one yellow square to make a four-patch unit. Press. Make 2 units for each block (40 total).

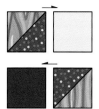

Make 40.

6. Join two corner units and two four-patch units to make one Hovering Hawks block. Press. Refer to the illustrations below for color placement and block quantities.

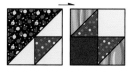 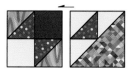 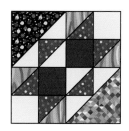

Make 16.

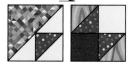 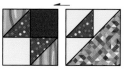 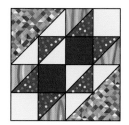

Make 4.

King's Crown Blocks

1. Referring to the directions on page 24 for making flying-geese units, join two rust dot 3" squares to one yellow rectangle to make one side unit. Press. Make 4 side units for each block (64 total).

Make 64.

2. Join four side units, four yellow 3" squares, and one geometric print square into rows. Press. Join rows to make one King's Crown block. Press. Make 16 blocks.

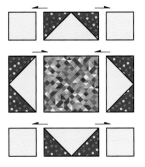
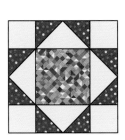

Make 16.

Quilt-Top Assembly

1. Arrange the Hovering Hawks and King's Crown blocks as shown and sew the blocks together in six rows of six blocks each. Press.

2. Referring to "Borders with Overlapped Corners" on pages 25–26, measure and cut the border strips and sew them to the side edges of the quilt top first, and then to the top and bottom edges. Press.

Finishing

1. Referring to "Layering the Quilt" on pages 28–29, layer the quilt top with batting and backing. Baste.

2. Referring to "Quilting" on page 29, quilt diagonal lines in both directions and stippling in the border.

3. Referring to "Squaring Up a Quilt" on page 31, square up the quilt sandwich.

4. Referring to "Binding" on pages 31–32, prepare and sew the binding to the quilt.

Alternate Fabric Plan

Notice the change in position of the darkest value and the addition of a floral border for a dramatically different look.

"Floral Splendor"

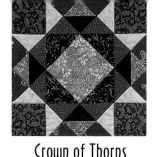

Crown of Thorns   Hour Glass Square

GOLDEN BOUGH

Materials

Yardage is based on 42"-wide fabric.

- 2⅜ yards of black print A for Crown of Thorns blocks, outer border, and binding
- 1½ yards of red print A for Crown of Thorns blocks, Hour Glass Square blocks, and inner border
- 1 yard of gold print for Crown of Thorns blocks and inner border
- ⅝ yard of cream print A for Crown of Thorns blocks
- ½ yard of red print B for Crown of Thorns blocks
- ½ yard of black print B for Crown of Thorns blocks
- ½ yard of black-and-green print for Crown of Thorns blocks
- ½ yard of cream print B for Hour Glass Square blocks
- ½ yard of tan print for Hour Glass Square blocks
- ⅜ yard of yellow print for Crown of Thorns blocks
- ⅜ yard of black print C for Hour Glass Square blocks
- ⅜ yard of brown print for Hour Glass Square blocks
- 4 yards of fabric for backing
- 66" x 66" piece of batting

Cutting

All measurements include ¼" seam allowances.

From black print A, cut in order:

7 strips, 2" x 42", from the crosswise grain

4 strips, 5" x the remaining lengthwise grain

1 piece, 18" x 21", from the remaining width

From the gold print, cut in order:

6 strips, 1¾" x 42"; crosscut into four 1¾" x 13" rectangles, four 1¾" x 14¼" rectangles, and four 1¾" x 15½" rectangles

1 piece, 18" x 21"

2 squares, 3¾" x 3¾"; cut each square twice diagonally to yield 8 quarter-square triangles

1 square, 9" x 9"

From red print A, cut:

5 strips, 3⅜" x 42"; crosscut into 48 squares, 3⅜" x 3⅜". Cut each square once diagonally to yield 96 half-square triangles.

2 pieces, 18" x 21"

1 square, 9" x 9"

From cream print A, cut:

2 pieces, 18" x 21"

From red print B, cut:

3 strips, 3¾" x 42"; crosscut into 26 squares, 3¾" x 3¾". Cut each square twice diagonally to yield 104 quarter-square triangles.

"Golden Bough" by Nancy Mahoney. Machine quilted by Jan Ogg. The red fabric acts as a bridge across the Crown of Thorns and Hour Glass Square blocks, producing a delightful design of stars and squares.

Finished Quilt Size: 62" x 62" ■ *Finished Block Size: 10"*

Golden Bough

FABRIC KEY

Crown of Thorns

Hour Glass Square

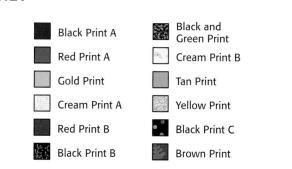

- Black Print A
- Red Print A
- Gold Print
- Cream Print A
- Red Print B
- Black Print B
- Black and Green Print
- Cream Print B
- Tan Print
- Yellow Print
- Black Print C
- Brown Print

From black print B, cut:

3 strips, 3⅜" x 42"; crosscut into 26 squares, 3⅜" x 3⅜". Cut each square once diagonally to yield 52 half-square triangles.

From the yellow print, cut:

2 strips, 4" x 42"; crosscut into 13 squares, 4" x 4"

From the black-and-green print, cut:

4 strips, 3" x 42"; crosscut into 52 squares, 3" x 3"

From the tan print, cut:

3 strips, 4⅜" x 42"; crosscut into 24 squares, 4⅜" x 4⅜". Cut each square once diagonally to yield 48 half-square triangles.

From the brown print, cut:

2 strips, 4⅜" x 42"; crosscut into 12 squares, 4⅜" x 4⅜". Cut each square once diagonally to yield 24 half-square triangles.

From black print C, cut:

2 strips, 4⅜" x 42"; crosscut into 12 squares, 4⅜" x 4⅜". Cut each square once diagonally to yield 24 half-square triangles.

From cream print B, cut:

4 strips, 3" x 42"; crosscut into 48 squares, 3" x 3"

Crown of Thorns Blocks

1. Pair the 18" x 21" piece of black print A with the 18" x 21" piece of gold print, right sides facing up. Cut and piece 2¼"-wide bias strips, following the directions on page 22 for making half-square-triangle units. Make two strip sets. Cut 52 half-square-triangle units, each 2¼" x 2¼".

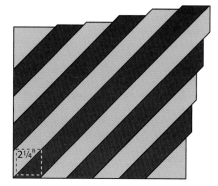

Make 2 strip sets.
Cut 52 units.

2. Pair each 18" x 21" piece of red print A with each 18" x 21" piece of cream print A, right sides facing up. Cut and piece 3¼"-wide bias strips, following the directions on page 22 for making half-square-triangle units. Make four strip sets. Cut 52

half-square-triangle units, each 3⅜" x 3⅜". Referring to "Quarter-Square-Triangle Units" on page 24, crosscut on the diagonal to yield 104 quarter-square-triangle units.

Make 4 strip sets.
Cut 52 units.

Make 104.

3. Join two red print B triangles to one black-and-gold half-square-triangle unit. Press. Add two quarter-square-triangle units to complete a side unit. Press. Make 52 total.

Make 52.

4. Join four black print B triangles to one yellow 4" square to make a center unit. Press. Make 13 total.

Make 13.

5. Join four black-and-green squares, four side units, and one center unit into rows. Press. Join rows to make one Crown of Thorns block. Press. Make 13 blocks.

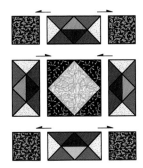

Make 13.

Hour Glass Square Blocks

1. Join one tan print 4⅜" triangle and one brown print 4⅜" triangle to make a half-square-triangle unit. Make 24 total. Join one tan print 4⅜" triangle and one black print C 4⅜" triangle to make a half-square-triangle unit. Make 24 total.

Make 24.

Make 24.

2. Join two tan-and-brown half-square-triangle units and two tan-and-black half-square-triangle units to make one center unit. Press. Make 12 total.

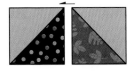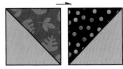

Make 12.

3. Join two red print A 3⅜" triangles to a cream print B square to make one corner unit. Press. Make 48 total.

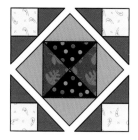

Make 48.

4. Join four corner units and one center unit to make one Hour Glass Square block. Press. Make 12 blocks.

Make 12.

Quilt-Top Assembly

1. Arrange and sew the blocks together in five rows of five blocks each, alternating the Crown of Thorns and Hour Glass Square blocks. Press.

NOTE: The quilt top must measure 50½" x 50½" at this point for the pieced border to fit properly.

2. For the inner-border strips, refer to "Half-Square-Triangle Units" on page 22. Pair the 9" square of red print A with the 9" square of gold print, right sides facing up. Cut and piece 3¼"-wide bias strips. Make two strip sets. Cut eight half-square-triangle units, each 3⅜" x 3⅜". Crosscut each unit on the diagonal to yield 16 quarter-square-triangle units. Refer to "Quarter-Square-Triangle Units" on page 24. Trim each gold triangle in the units to measure 1¾".

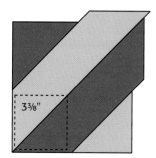

3⅜"

Make 2 strip sets.
Cut 8 units.

1¾"

3. Join two quarter-square-triangle units to one gold triangle to make one border unit. Press. Make eight total.

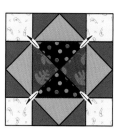

Make 8.

4. Join two gold 1¾" x 13" rectangles, one gold 1¾" x 15½" rectangle, and two border units to make one side inner-border strip. Press. Repeat.

13"   15½"   13"

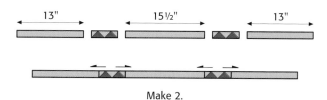

Make 2.

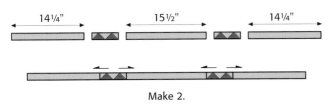

5. Join two gold 1¾" x 14¼" rectangles, one gold 1¾" x 15½" rectangle, and two border units to make the top inner-border strip. Press. Repeat for the bottom inner-border strip.

14¼"   15½"   14¼"

Make 2.

6. Referring to "Borders with Overlapped Corners" on pages 25–26, sew the inner-border strips to the side edges of the quilt top first, and then to the top and bottom edges. Press.

7. Referring to "Borders with Overlapped Corners," measure and cut the outer-border strips and sew them to the side edges of the quilt top first, and then to the top and bottom edges. Press.

Finishing

1. Referring to "Layering the Quilt" on pages 28–29, layer the quilt top with batting and backing. Baste.

2. Referring to "Quilting" on page 29, quilt straight lines in the ditch and with a motif over the Hour Glass Square blocks.

3. Referring to "Squaring Up a Quilt" on page 31, square up the quilt sandwich.

4. Referring to "Binding" on pages 31–32, prepare and sew the binding to the quilt.

Alternate Fabric Plan

Achieve a new secondary design by reversing the position of the light- and dark-value fabrics.

"Free Spirit"

World's Fair

Hour Glass Square

Black Magic

Materials

Yardage is based on 42"-wide fabric.

- 3 yards of black floral for World's Fair blocks, Hour Glass Square blocks, outer border, and binding
- 2⅝ yards of yellow print for World's Fair blocks, Hour Glass Square blocks, and inner border
- 1¼ yards of tan-and-plum print for World's Fair and Hour Glass Square blocks
- ¾ yard of plum print for World's Fair blocks
- ⅝ yard of black-and-green print for Hour Glass Square blocks
- ½ yard of green print for World's Fair blocks
- 4¾ yards of fabric for backing
- 77" x 77" piece of batting

Cutting

All measurements include ¼" seam allowances.

From the tan-and-plum print, cut:

4 strips, 5⅛" x 42"; crosscut into 24 squares, 5⅛" x 5⅛". Cut each square once diagonally to yield 48 half-square triangles.

2 pieces, 18" x 21"

From the yellow print, cut:

5 strips, 1⅝" x 42"; using template A (page 94), cut 52 pieces

2 strips, 5⅛" x 42"; crosscut into 12 squares, 5⅛" x 5⅛". Cut each square once diagonally to yield 24 half-square triangles.

5 strips, 3⅞" x 42"; crosscut into 48 squares, 3⅞" x 3⅞". Cut each square once diagonally to yield 96 half-square triangles.

3 strips, 4¼" x 42"; crosscut into 26 squares, 4¼" x 4¼". Cut each square twice diagonally to yield 104 quarter-square triangles.

7 strips, 2" x 42"

2 pieces, 18" x 21"

From the black floral, cut in order:

2 strips, 4¾" x 42", from the crosswise grain; crosscut into 13 squares, 4¾" x 4¾"

8 strips, 2" x 42", from the crosswise grain

4 strips, 5" x the remaining lengthwise grain

10 strips, 2¾" x the remaining width of fabric; using template B (page 94), cut 104 pieces

12 squares, 5⅛" x 5⅛", from the remaining width of fabric; cut each square once diagonally to yield 24 half-square triangles.

From the plum print, cut:

5 strips, 1⅝" x 42"; using template A (page 94), cut 52 pieces

4 strips, 3" x 42"; crosscut into 52 squares, 3" x 3". Cut each square once diagonally to yield 104 half-square triangles.

From the green print, cut:

4 strips, 2⅝" x 42"; crosscut into 52 squares, 2⅝" x 2⅝"

From the black-and-green print, cut:

5 strips, 3½" x 42"; crosscut into 48 squares, 3½" x 3½"

"Black Magic" by Nancy Mahoney. Machine quilted by Susan Powell. The gold background fabric successfully blends the World's Fair and Hour Glass Square to create a magical overall design.

Finished Quilt Size: 72½" x 72½" ■ *Finished Block Size: 12"*

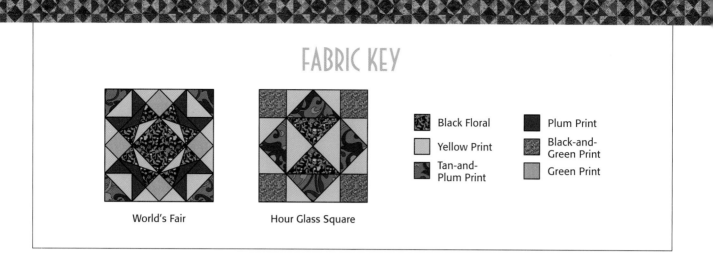

World's Fair   Hour Glass Square

Black Floral   Plum Print

Yellow Print   Black-and-
                      Green Print

Tan-and-   Green Print
Plum Print

World's Fair Blocks

1. Pair each 18" x 21" piece of tan-and-plum print with each 18" x 21" piece of yellow print, right sides facing up. Cut and piece 3"-wide bias strips, following the directions on page 22 for making half-square-triangle units. Make 3 strip sets. Cut 52 half-square-triangle units, each 3½" x 3½".

3½"

Make 3 strip sets.
Cut 52 units.

2. Join one black floral piece cut with template B to one plum piece cut with template A. Press. Join one black floral piece cut with template B to one yellow piece cut with template A. Press. Join the two pieces to make a rectangle unit. Make 4 units for each block (52 total).

Make 52.

3. Join two yellow 4¼" triangles to one green square to make one side unit. Press. Make 4 units for each block (52 total).

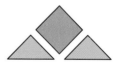

Make 52.

4. Join two plum 3" triangles to one half-square-triangle unit to make one corner unit. Press. Make 4 units for each block (52 total).

Make 52.

5. Join four rectangle units, four side units, four corner units, and one black floral 4¾" square to make one World's Fair block. Press. Make 13 blocks.

Make 13.

Hour Glass Square Blocks

1. Join one yellow 5⅛" triangle to one tan-and-plum triangle to make a half-square-triangle unit. Press. Make 24 total. Join one black floral 5⅛" triangle to one tan-and-plum triangle to make a half-square-triangle unit. Press. Make 24 total.

Make 24.

Make 24.

2. Join two yellow-tan-and-plum half-square-triangle units and two black-floral-tan-and-plum half-square-triangle units to make one center unit. Press. Make 12 total.

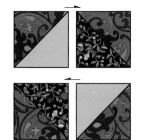

Make 12.

3. Join two yellow 3⅞" triangles and one black-and-green square to make one corner unit. Press. Make 4 units for each block (48 total).

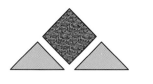

Make 48.

4. Join one center unit and four corner units to make one Hour Glass Square block. Press. Make 12 blocks.

Make 12.

Quilt-Top Assembly

1. Arrange and sew the blocks together in five rows of five blocks each, alternating the World's Fair blocks and Hour Glass Square blocks. Press.

2. Referring to "Borders with Overlapped Corners" on pages 25–26, measure and cut the 2"-wide inner-border strips and sew them to the side edges of the quilt top first, and then to the top and bottom edges. Press. Repeat for the outer border. Press.

Finishing

1. Referring to "Layering the Quilt" on pages 28–29, layer the quilt top with batting and backing. Baste.

2. Referring to "Quilting" on page 29, quilt the World's Fair blocks in the ditch and a motif over the Hour Glass Square blocks.

3. Referring to "Squaring Up a Quilt" on page 31, square up the quilt sandwich.

4. Referring to "Binding" on pages 31–32, prepare and sew the binding to the quilt.

Alternate Quilt Plan

See the new secondary design generated by the addition of a light background fabric.

"Hazelnut Latte"

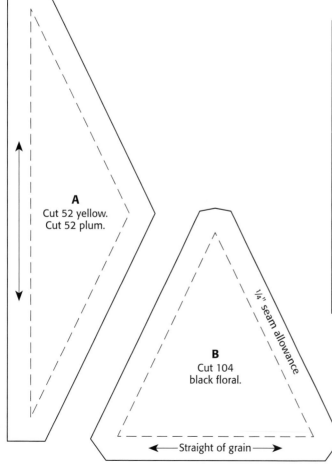

A
Cut 52 yellow.
Cut 52 plum.

¼" seam allowance

B
Cut 104
black floral.

◄— Straight of grain —►

ABOUT THE AUTHOR

Nancy Mahoney is an enthusiastic quiltmaker, teacher, fabric designer, and author. Her first book, *Rich Traditions*, was also published by Martingale & Company. She enjoys speaking at quilt guilds and meeting other quilters, especially beginning quilters.

Nancy has been actively quilting since 1987, after taking a scrap quilt class from Marsha McCloskey. The quilt from Marsha's class was included in the book *A Dozen Variables* by Marsha and Nancy J. Martin. Nancy's quilts have been in many quilt books as well as a number of national quilt magazines. Her quilts have also won many awards, including two first-place ribbons. She enjoys the art of quiltmaking, and she believes that making beautiful quilts is fun. She also feels that each quilt is an exciting learning experience. She finds inspiration for quilt designs in everything she sees, including everyday objects, nature, and vintage quilts.

After living twenty years in Seattle, Washington, Nancy now makes her home in Palm Coast, Florida. When she's not quilting, she enjoys gardening, walking on the beach, and shopping for antiques.

new and bestselling titles from

America's Best-Loved Craft & Hobby Books®

America's Best-Loved Quilt Books®

NEW RELEASES
1000 Great Quilt Blocks
Basically Brilliant Knits
Bright Quilts from Down Under
Christmas Delights
Creative Machine Stitching
Crochet for Tots
Crocheted Aran Sweaters
Cutting Corners
Everyday Embellishments
Folk Art Friends
Garden Party
Hocus Pocus!
Just Can't Cut It!
Quilter's Home: Winter, The
Sweet and Simple Baby Quilts
Time to Quilt
Today's Crochet
Traditional Quilts to Paper Piece

APPLIQUÉ
Appliquilt in the Cabin
Artful Album Quilts
Artful Appliqué
Blossoms in Winter
Color-Blend Appliqué
Sunbonnet Sue All through the Year

BABY QUILTS
Easy Paper-Pieced Baby Quilts
Even More Quilts for Baby
More Quilts for Baby
Play Quilts
Quilted Nursery, The
Quilts for Baby

HOLIDAY QUILTS & CRAFTS
Christmas Cats and Dogs
Creepy Crafty Halloween
Handcrafted Christmas, A
Make Room for Christmas Quilts
Welcome to the North Pole

HOME DECORATING
Decorated Kitchen, The
Decorated Porch, The
Dresden Fan
Gracing the Table
Make Room for Quilts
Quilts for Mantels and More
Sweet Dreams

LEARNING TO QUILT
101 Fabulous Rotary-Cut Quilts
Beyond the Blocks
Casual Quilter, The
Feathers That Fly
Joy of Quilting, The
Simple Joys of Quilting, The
Your First Quilt Book (or it should be!)

PAPER PIECING
40 Bright and Bold Paper-Pieced Blocks
50 Fabulous Paper-Pieced Stars
For the Birds
Quilter's Ark, A
Rich Traditions
Split-Diamond Dazzlers

ROTARY CUTTING
365 Quilt Blocks a Year Perpetual Calendar
Around the Block Again
Around the Block with Judy Hopkins
Fat Quarter Quilts
More Fat Quarter Quilts
Stack the Deck!
Triangle Tricks
Triangle-Free Quilts

SCRAP QUILTS
Nickel Quilts
Scrap Frenzy
Scrappy Duos
Spectacular Scraps
Strips and Strings
Successful Scrap Quilts

TOPICS IN QUILTMAKING
American Stenciled Quilts
Americana Quilts
Batik Beauties
Bed and Breakfast Quilts
Fabulous Quilts from Favorite Patterns
Frayed-Edge Fun
Patriotic Little Quilts
Reversible Quilts

CRAFTS
ABCs of Making Teddy Bears, The
Blissful Bath, The
Handcrafted Frames
Handcrafted Garden Accents
Handprint Quilts
Painted Chairs
Painted Whimsies

KNITTING & CROCHET
365 Knitting Stitches a Year Perpetual
    Calendar
Clever Knits
Crochet for Babies and Toddlers
Crocheted Sweaters
Knitted Sweaters for Every Season
Knitted Throws and More
Knitter's Book of Finishing Techniques, Th
Knitter's Template, A
More Paintbox Knits
Paintbox Knits
Too Cute! Cotton Knits for Toddlers
Treasury of Rowan Knits, A
Ultimate Knitter's Guide, The

Our books are available at bookstores and your favorite craft, fabric, and yarn retailers. If you don't see the title you're looking for, visit us at **www.martingale-pub.com** or contact us at:

1-800-426-3126

International: 1-425-483-3313

Fax: 1-425-486-7596

Email: info@martingale-pub.com

For more information and a full list of our titles, visit our Web site.
